Issue 4 December 2000

Masculinities

Special Issue

Edited by Christopher Breward

Edited by Dr. Valerie Steele

Fashion Theory

The Journal of Dress, Body & Culture

BERG

Fashion Theory: The Journal of Dress, Body & Culture

Editor
Dr. Valerie Steele
The Museum at the Fashion Institute of Technology, E201
Seventh Avenue at 27th Street
New York, NY 10001-5992
USA
Fax: +1 212 924 3958
e-mail: steelemajor@earthlink.net

Book Reviews Editor
Christopher Breward
The London College of Fashion
20 John Princes Street
London W1M 0BJ

Please send all books for review to the Book Reviews Editor.

Aims and Scope
The importance of studying the body as a site for the deployment of discourses is well-established in a number of disciplines. By contrast, the study of fashion has, until recently, suffered from a lack of critical analysis. Increasingly, however, scholars have recognized the cultural significance of self-fashioning, including not only clothing but also such body alterations as tattooing and piercing. *Fashion Theory* takes as its starting point a definition of 'fashion' as the cultural construction of the embodied identity. It aims to provide an interdisciplinary forum for the rigorous analysis of cultural phenomena ranging from footbinding to fashion advertising.

Anyone wishing to submit an article, interview, or a book, film or exhibition review for possible publication in this journal should contact Valerie Steele (at the address listed to the left) or the Editorial Department at Berg (150 Cowley Road, Oxford, OX4 1JJ, UK; e-mail: enquiry@berg.demon.co.uk).

Notes for Contributors can be found at the back of the journal.

ISSN: 1362-704X

Ordering Information
Four issues per volume. One volume per annum. 2000: Volume 4

By mail:
Berg Publishers,
150 Cowley Road,
Oxford,
OX4 1JJ,
UK.

By fax: +44 (0) 1865 791165

By telephone: +44 (0) 1865 245104

By e-mail: enquiry@berg.demon.co.uk

Inquiries
Editorial: Kathryn Earle, Managing Editor, e-mail: kearle@berg1.demon.co.uk

Production: Sara Everett, e-mail: severett@berg.demon.co.uk

Advertising + subscriptions: enquiry@berg.demon.co.uk

Subscription Rates:
Institutional base list subscription price: £86.00, US$140.00.
Individuals' subscription price: £35.00, US$55.00.

Reprints of Individual Articles
Copies of individual articles may be obtained from the Publishers at the appropriate fees. Write to: Berg, 150 Cowley Road, Oxford, OX4 1JJ, UK.

Printed in the United Kingdom.
DECEMBER 2000

Indexed by the International Bibliography of Social Sciences; The MLA International Bibliography; ARTbibliographies and Clothing and Textile Arts Index

Page 373

Page 405

Page 427

Page 487

Contents

Editor
Dr. Valerie Steele
The Museum at the Fashion Institute of Technology, E201
Seventh Avenue at 27th Street
New York, NY 10001-5992
USA

Fax +1 212 924 3958
e-mail: steelemajor@earthlink.net

BERG

Fashion Theory, Volume 4, Issue 4, pp.371–372
Reprints available directly from the Publishers.
Photocopying permitted by licence only.

Letter from the Editor

Over the past two decades we have seen reams of paper devoted to the study of an assumed crisis in masculine identities in the West. In British cultural and media studies especially, the successive rise of the "New Man" during the 1980s and his bastard progeny, the "New Lad" in the 1990s has been used to account for a whole range of societal phenomena. From the political fall-out of second-wave feminism to the proliferation of glossy lifestyle magazines the reactive strategies of young men have drawn unprecedented academic and popular attention. Fashionable identities in particular have been positioned in the center of the field and consumption isolated as the primary practice through which new forms of masculinity have staked their position in culture and representation. It is both in response to the usefulness of this expanding literature and a sense of frustration at some of the assumptions which it makes that this special issue of *Fashion Theory* was proposed.

On the first count all of the articles collected here assume that masculinity as a social identity is entirely contingent on historical circumstances and that its varied characteristics work both at the level of representation and through the physical trappings of material culture, especially clothing. Like the most interesting work in recent studies of gender and representation they argue for a theory of masculinity that prioritizes the shifting surfaces of fashionable life as a productive motor for challenging new subject positions. On the second count the articles work against the prevailing assumption that many of the debates around masculinity and lifestyle are of recent origin. Those of us working on the broad development of fashion are familiar with the constant claims of other historians that "their" periods bore sole witness to processes of revolution and "crisis." The joy of dress as a historical tool is that its internal mechanisms and cultural affiliations suggest a constant state of change. To isolate one historical moment over another as the birth of, for example, consumer culture or the demise of the working-class is to misrepresent the complex influences that dictate our fragmented experience of modernity. What these articles offer are snapshots, through the medium of fashion, of the ways in which previous generations of men continually found their aspirations and self-knowledge challenged by new technologies, developments in the rule of taste and shifting social or political responsibilities. The "New Man" it turns out is not so "New" at all; his physical trappings and sartorial anxieties echo back through the years to the Macaroni of the 1770s and possibly beyond.

In terms of method all of the articles benefit from their close attention to very specific moments and contexts. Most are not theoretical in the abstract or critical sense of the word but attempt (in a common approach to history that is nevertheless productively "theorized") to analyze the ongoing relationship of groups of men to their clothes through a careful reading of appropriate archives. The range of sources drawn upon is wide and as a whole the special edition shows how surviving dress, literary description, caricature, retail ephemera, biography, journalism and film can all be brought to bear in describing aspects of masculine fashionability that would otherwise be lost to the record. For reasons of consistency and focus we have decided to concentrate here on specific manifestations of manly consumption as they occurred in England and America between the eighteenth and mid-twentieth centuries. There is much more to be said about masculinities and fashion in a global context and in periods outside of the late-modern, but that perhaps requires a further special issue! In the meantime I would like to thank all of the contributors for the exemplary attention to scholarship that they displayed during the writing and editing process and to offer my gratitude to Valerie Steele and Kathryn Earle for giving over this space for a consideration of an important and growing aspect of fashion studies. I hope it inspires future work.

Christopher Breward

Fashion Theory, Volume 4, Issue 4, pp.373–404
Reprints available directly from the Publishers.
Photocopying permitted by licence only.

Macaroni Masculinities[1]

Peter McNeil

Peter McNeil wrote his Ph.D. (University of Sydney 1999) on the subject of costume and the macaroni. He has published articles in journals including *Art History, Fashion Theory* and *Journal of Design History*. He is Lecturer in Design History and Theory at College of Fine Arts, University of New South Wales.

This article discusses aspects of the macaroni persona and phenomenon, with reference to transformations of masculinity and gendered consumption in eighteenth-century London. It considers the way in which the dress prerogatives of the male elite may have passed into the reach of the "lower" orders, as cast-offs and cheaper versions circulating within the burgeoning fashion economy. As the English macaroni was wearing contemporary courtly fashion, but in a particular social climate and in a particular way, it can be argued that macaronic behavior is more about the wearing, less about the "worn"; more about the process, less about the product. This is, of course, true of all fashion; but the macaroni provides a particularly apt and pronounced case-study of this issue. In this essay I also argue for an alternative or additional derivation of the term "macaroni" that privileges this very sense of performative burlesque. In these terms, the relevant suits and waistcoats that rest in museums are inanimate leftovers of a performance of a particular type of masculinity. The essay thus makes a case for the benefits of a cultural studies approach to eighteenth-century male dress, in which the relationship between modernity, fashion and representation is foregrounded, and macaroni dress related to evolving models of national and gendered identity.

The "Macaroni": Definitions and Derivations

In 1823, when the revised edition of Pierce Egan's *Grose's Classical Dictionary of the Vulgar Tongue* included the term "macaroni," it had been circulating in the English language for some sixty years, to denote a type of fop:

> Maccaroni [*sic*], An Italian paste made of flour and eggs; also, a fop; which name arose from a club, called the Maccaroni [*sic*] Club, instituted by some of the most dressy travelled gentlemen about town, who led the fashions; whence a man foppishly dressed was supposed a member of that club, and, by contradiction, stiled [*sic*] a Maccaroni [*sic*] (Egan 1823).

An explanation similar to Grose's dictionary entry has been reiterated whenever historians seek an explanation for the meaning and resonance of this expression. A review of the primary sources on which historians of eighteenth-century culture, dress and manners have formulated their understanding of the macaroni indicates that many definitions of the macaroni found in scholarly and popular texts today are flawed or partial. To reiterate the explanations for the term found in the eighteenth-century press, as some historians have done, is problematic. Useful and amusing as these descriptions are, they occur in the context of a genre that was ironic, arch and designed to amuse. The story of the pasta-eating club is possibly apocryphal; it made a convenient contrast with the real beefsteak club and the symbolic roast beef of England, which in discourse represented nationalism rather than internationalism; the values of liberty and free speech versus absolutism and tyranny. Such fictional clubs circulated in eighteenth-century literature and the press to underline a moral point and satirize pretension and outlandish behavior. Their use belongs to an older tradition that dates to the early years of the century (Allen 1967 and Chancellor n.d.). No scholar has provided evidence of the existence of a concrete club with members and premises. Clues presented in later memoirs and biographies that discussed macaroni figures are ambiguous on this point (Stirling 1911: 323). It therefore is difficult to ascertain whether a discrete club existed with its own rules and premises, or if the macaroni coterie was situated within the structure of an existing club such as Almack's. Whether the macaroni 'club' existed or not is on one level not so important as that it circulated within contemporary discourse as a vital piece of popular culture.

Horace Walpole and the "Maccaroni" Club

It is generally accepted by scholars of costume and social history that the first recorded use of the term "macaroni" occurs amongst the voluminous correspondence of Horace Walpole, although this is not strictly true. The word "macaroni" as a reference to appearance and character predates Walpole's letters and appears in David Garrick's play, *The Male-Coquette* (1757), which included a foppish character called the Marchese di Macaroni. Miles Ogborn describes Marcourt in George Colman's *Man and Wife* (1770) as the "first Macaroni character on stage" (Ogborn 1998: 139). That a "maccaroni" [*sic*] was also later included in Garrick's *Bon Ton* (1775) indicates the currency of this type within contemporary comedy. Despite its theatrical predecessor, Walpole's piercing eye and trenchant prose did record the first detailed impression of the macaroni phenomenon when it appeared amongst the aristocracy in London. Revealing the topicality and the specific nature of his theme—as not just a "fop" but a new social type of conspicuous dresser—Walpole discusses the macaroni as if he were a novelty. In the first relevant letter, dated 6 February 1764, addressed to Lord Hertford, Walpole discussed gambling losses amongst the sons of foreign aristocrats at the "Maccaroni [*sic*] club, which is composed of all the travelled young men who wear long curls and spying-glasses" (Lewis 1937–83 vol. 38: 306). Contained here are many of the elements of the macaroni stereotype that would circulate extensively in the London press, satirical prints and plays of the 1770s.

Walpole's "travelled young men" clearly refers to those aristocrats who had taken the Grand Tour; in the context of this quote he is referring to a group of youths comprising either French or Swiss and Modenese aristocrats, a thoroughly cosmopolitan gaming table. These were the Duc de Chaulne's son; "Virette" (possibly Vivret, a Swiss or Genevan); the Marchese Giuseppe Paolucci, Modenese envoy to England; and the Duc de Pecquigny. Walpole records the names as worthy of note because a feud broke out over the payment of gaming debts (Lewis 1937–83 vol. 38: 306, notes 4–5). Profligate gambling, associated with continental and specifically French manners, was strongly associated with the macaronic type, and was itself the focus of much critical literature. Gaming was highly fashionable and losses had reached epidemic proportions. Charles James Fox's stakes of £3,000, and total gambling debts of £140,000, were public knowledge, included in macaroni ditties and satires (Walpole 1806: 23 and Trevelyan 1880: 484). As in France, the behavior was widely reported and associated in the public mind with the decadence of a spent aristocracy. Matthew and Mary Darly included *A Macaroni Gambler* in their third suite of macaroni caricatures, a topical image that referred to Alexander Fordyce, a Scottish banker who enjoyed the misfortune of having a name exceptionally apt for punning. *The Macaroni Card Players*, a group of ladies and gentlemen, was published as an illustration in *The Macaroni, Scavoir* [sic] *Vivre, and Theatrical Magazine*, November 1773.

Walpole's "spying-glass" refers to a monocle in a decorative setting; the expensive glass sets the holder off from the crowd, casting him as an observer and by extension an outsider. The reference to "long curls" is perhaps the most significant; fashionable young men in the late 1760s and 1770s replaced the small scratch-wig of the older generation with elaborate hairstyles that matched the towering heights of the female *coiffure*. A tall *toupée* and a club of hair required extensive dressing with pomade and powder. The wig was garnished with a large black satin wig-bag trimmed with bows. The use of a long pig-tail and wig-bag was viewed as a Francophile affectation; so much so that the visual shorthand for all Frenchmen in popular imagery was this device, just as a Dutchman was dressed in clogs and a Spaniard in lace. It was the macaronic attention to wigs that caused the most consternation. As Marcia Pointon so deftly indicates in *Hanging the Head*, the wig can function as a sign of masculinity and masculine authority; men without their wig or with their wig slipping are used in images to suggest disempowerment or castration (Pointon 1993: 117–23). In the engraving *Two Bloods of Humour, returning from the Bagnio, after having Kept it Up* (British Museum), the drunken figures roar: "I SAY KEEP IT UP-KEEP IT UP—'TIS LIFE MY BOY—SO LET'S KEEP IT UP [*sic*]." The parallel of the erect wig and potency is stressed in that one of them has the wig placed on backwards, so that the hind part hangs over his face. The type of the wig dictated the response; effeminate excess was alarming. Macaronies in popular imagery are tailed by hairdressers with devil-like horns and hideous physiognomies; they are mercilessly lampooned as partners in crime, often effete, wizened and satanic. The cost of these wigs might also have excited dismay; even a modest wig was amongst the most expensive items in a gentleman's wardrobe. The macaroni wig was thus a sign of conspicuous consumption and luxury. If not the clothing, then the general effect of a macaronic hair-style would have been possible to replicate; although wigs were very expensive, real hair could be dressed in the new manner and augmented with false, and there was a trade in second-hand and stolen wigs (Pointon 1993: 120). The ragged-looking confections thrust on the heads of many caricatured individuals in the Darlys' macaroni engravings suggest ridiculous efforts to follow an inherently expensive fashion. Not knowing what was real and what was false was part of the alarm excited by fashion. The wig's symbolism as a potentially deceitful object is indicated in the following incident from the diary of Sophie Von La Roche, 1786. An English customs official she described as "Hogarthian" (even at this date the English scene was mediated through caricature imagery) insisted upon inspecting the wig-box of a fellow traveller:

> The customs man raised his voice, flashed his eyes with greater fire, and insisted on opening the box; then, looking important meanwhile, lifted out the wig, lying there in blissful content, and dropped it again scornfully. The foreigner said, "It is only my wig after all, isn't it?' "Yes," he replied, "but a wig often covers a multitude of sins" (S. Roche 1933: 80).

Although the existence of the Macaroni club has been freely assumed by several historians of dress, and by the editor of the encyclopedic Walpole correspondence, none has provided any further proof of its membership or premises.[2] The Macaroni club is always something heard of, not entered, and even Walpole does not name its location. Had Walpole known more it would have been uncharacteristic for such a "voluptuary of gossip" (Tillyard 1994: 12) not to detail its structure and members, in accordance with his penchant for passing on gossip to posterity. As the contemporary press printed articles making similar claims in 1772 (*Town and Country* 1772: 242–3), subsequent historians have tended to accept this explanation of the term. The Edwardian biographer of the macaroni, Walter Stanhope, wrote that the dish macaroni was "always placed on the table at their dinners." Although the scholar had access to Stanhope's papers, he did not note the source of this claim (Stirling 1911: 323). The club Walpole refers to is possibly his amalgam of all the fashionable clubs in St James's Street, and thus indicative of youthful fashionability generally, or one of two clubs known to have been frequented by macaronies such as Charles James Fox. The first is the Robert Adam-designed Boodle's, also known as the "Savoir Vivre," where vast fortunes were spent gambling by men including the Fox brothers. The second contender is Almack's. Brooks's, the Whig club attended by Sheridan, Fox and the Prince of Wales and set up to rival Almack's on the opposite side of the street, was not fully established until 1778 (Ayling 1991: 49). Walpole linked Almack's with macaronies several times in his correspondence; there were "Macaronis lolling out of windows at Almack's like carpets to be dusted" (Lewis 1937–83 vol. 35: 458). The *Macaroni and Theatrical Magazine* also referred to Almack's, describing: "a compound dish of vermicelli and other pastes, which, unknown in England until then, was imported by our Connoscenti [*sic*] in eating, as an improvement to their subscription table at Almack's" (Stephens and Hawkins 1883: 826). If one had to "gamble" on the site of the macaroni club, Almack's is thus the most likely contender. The issue of the club established an aristocratic profile for the macaroni when he first appeared. By the 1730s, clubs were in part political, the dual *raison d'être* being represented in the title of the Rumpsteak or Liberty Club (1734), which positioned itself in opposition to Robert Walpole's government. Other clubs included the

Mohawks; the Society for the Propagation of Sicilian Amorology; the Wet Paper Brigade, which supposedly read the papers damp from the presses; the Lying Club; the Ugly Club; the Hell-fire Club; and the Dilettanti Society. Walpole's description of the macaroni club is designed to amuse his correspondents, who were familiar with the ambience of Whig establishments, notorious for gaming, feasting and carousing.

Several other macaroni references enliven Walpole's letters in 1764. In November, he indicated that macaroni dress was a style associated with youth, when he observed at the Opera: "You see I am not likely, like my brother Cholmondeley . . . to totter into a solitaire at threescore" (Lewis 1937–83 vol. 38: 470). He reiterated this observation in 1775: "The macaronies will laugh out, for you say I am still in the fashionable world.—What! they will cry, as they read while their hair is curling,—that old soul;—for old and old-fashioned are synonymous in the vocabulary of mode, alas!" (Lewis 1937–83 vol. 28: 186). Macaroni color schemes for various seasons, probably copied from the vibrant combinations deployed in French fashions, and also resembling the preferred interior architectural schemes of Robert Adam, are indicated: "If I went to Almack's and decked out my wrinkles in pink and green like Lord Harrington, I might still be in vogue" (Lewis 1937–83 vol. 32: 191). In 1775, *Matrimonial Magazine* noted that "A few months ago most of the Macaronies had got into a sort of jaundiced habit; a kind of orange-tawney . . . and of late there has been a most *unseasonable* rage for GREEN CAPES [*sic*]" (Lewis 1937–83 vol. 32: 191, note 8).[3] This is borne out in two letters written by Samuel Johnson, in which he expresses an enthusiasm for this color scheme as well as a deep orange in that year:

> This day I had a new great Coat which am exceedingly pleas'd with; it is a light colour with a light green collar, made in the new fashion; the colour of the Coat depends on one's own fancy but the green Capes are almost universal . . .
>
> Went to Mr. Lane to talk about another Suit of Cloaths [*sic*] for a best Suit (I have since chosen a Barri [*sic*] colour, a colour deeper than an orange) from him (Radcliffe 1930: 40–1).

Such letters provide powerful evidence of the pleasures involved in the pursuit of macaroni fashion by young men.

Conspicuous "Waste"

Walpole's correspondence thus established the characteristics of the macaroni stereotype when he first appeared, and from the beginning linked the macaroni with the themes that provided part of the impetus for the scurrilous visual and verbal caricatures that were generated in their hundreds soon after. These comment on fashion and luxury at a time when those terms were the subject of theoretical and economic debate (Berry 1994). The connection in Walpole's mind between the macaroni and the extravagant Whig circle around Charles James Fox is presented in July 1773. The macaronies become a metaphor for problems with the currency and a draining of the economy:

> Ireland is drained and has not a shilling. The explosion of the Scotch banks has reduced them almost as low, and sunk their flourishing manufactures to low water ebb. The Maccaronis [*sic*] are at their *ne plus ultra*: Charles Fox is already so like Julius Caesar, that he owes an hundred thousand pounds . . . What is England now?—A sink of Indian wealth, filled by nabobs and emptied by Maccaronis! A senate sold and despised! A country over-run by horse-races! A gaming, robbing, wrangling, railing nation, without principles, genius, character or allies; the over-grown shadow of what it was! (Lewis 1937–83 vol. 23: 498–9).

Walpole, as usual, exaggerated; he continued: "Lord bless me, I run on like a political barber—I must go back to my shop . . ." (Lewis 1937–83 vol. 23: 499). His excessive speech pattern was itself drawn out as macaronic. Walpole revelled in peppering his correspondence with the current term; even the Summer arrives "*à la Maccaroni* three months too late" (Lewis 1937–83 vol. 32: 382). He referred to some women as "maccaronesses," but this was as suggestive of their propensity to gamble as their appearance; "the ladies are all Maccaronies and game too deep for me" (Lewis 1937–83 vol. 32: 158). The caricature industry also produced images of female macaronies, sometimes as part of a suite that paired male and female sartorial absurdity, as amusing counterpoint to the male macaroni, and as an extension of the link between women and vanity. Ultra-fashionable women were sometimes addressed by both actor and audience in the contemporary theater. In October 1775 in his cross-dressed role in *The Provoked Wife*, Garrick brought down the house with his feather head-dress: "Mr. G.—never play'd better, & when he was in Woman's Cloaths he had a head drest with Feathers, Fruit etc. as extravagant as possible to Burlesque the present Mode of Dressing—it had a Monstrous Effect" (Stone and Kahrl 1979: 497). A newspaper reported the head-dress included feathers, ribbons, oranges and lemons, and flowers: "The ladies in the boxes drew back their heads, as if ashamed of the picture" (Thomas 1989: 382). Similarly, Sophie Von La Roche described a group of ultra-fashionable women and fops literally driven from the theater by the combined attentions of actors and audience. A group of four ladies:

> entered a box during the third play, with such wonderfully fantastic caps and hats perched on their heads, that they were received by the entire audience with loud derision. Their neckerchiefs were

> puffed up so high that their noses were scarce visible, and their nosegays were like huge shrubs, large enough to conceal a person. In less than a quarter of an hour, when the scene had changed to a market-square in any case, four women walked on to the stage dressed equally foolishly, and hailed the four ladies in the box as their friends. All clapped loud applause. The two gentlemen accompanying the fashionable fools were least able to endure the scorn, for they hastily made away. One of the women held her fan before her face, and was thereupon called by name—and when the expression of the remarks became too strong, they too departed before the end of the sketch, but they were followed out by a number of people from the pit and gallery, and held up to ridicule (S. Roche 1933: 95).

A decade later, in his copy of Mason's *Heroic Epistle* (1777), Walpole mocked the word macaroni, stating that its very novelty was a symbol of the fashion system.

> Maccaroni is synonimous [*sic*] to Beau, Fop, Cox-comb, Petit Maître, &c. for Fashion having no foundation in Sense, or in the flower of sense, Taste, deals in forms & names, by altering which it thinks it invents. Maccaroni was a name adopted by or given to the young Men of fashion who returned from their Travels in the present reign, and is supposed to have been derived from the Italian paste of that denomination . . . The Chiefs of the Maccaronis [*sic*] became known beyond the limits of their fantastic Dominion by their excessive gaming . . . (Toynbee 1926: 69–70).

Language and money—two symbolic orders—are treated here by Walpole as mere self-reflexive systems. The words for "macaroni" were interchangeable; eighteenth-century writers and readers enjoyed the play of synonyms, an excess of signifiers. Excess detaches representation from its purportedly "real" signified in all cases; macaronies did the same with fashion. From the 1770s men's costume became increasingly self-referential. The elements of male attire—coat, waistcoat, breeches—remained unchanged for formal wear. However, various elements—fringe, frogging, braid, buckles, shoe-heels, hats—were manipulated as part of a sartorial language in neither logical order nor manner. Macaroni dressing thus has a strong relationship to the excesses typical of later *Incroyable* dress, a process hastened in post-Revolutionary France by the destruction of the hierarchical feudal system and its replacement by a society of *nouveaux-riches* composed of speculators or *agioteurs* who had no need of court-dress, but revelled in novel and extraordinary effects (Siegfried 1995: 70–81).

The macaroni's contemporary counterpart across the Channel, the *petit-maître*, was also manipulating clothing in such a way that bemused commentators could only describe it as a new age of ephemerality. *Petit maître* was perhaps the most common counterpart for "macaroni." The English also understood the macaroni in terms of this French courtier counterpart. In the mid-1770s, buttons on ultra-fashionable men's dress in France lost any functional role and became bizarrely distorted; the Comte d'Artois wore watches mounted as buttons; there were pornographic buttons on sale in the Palais-Royal, and rebus and alphabetical buttons of the type that had previously appeared on screens (Quicherat 1875: 604; d'Allemagne 1928, Vol. 1: 59). Some men changed their buttons several times a day; a set *à la Buffon* contained insects or leaves imprisoned in glass (Musée de la Mode et du Costume 1983: 117). By the 1780s, three, four or five *gilets* were worn on top of each other, waistcoats of "conspicuous waste" as Lesley and Osmun wittily noted, but also representative of the scrambling of the logic of fashion (Lesley and Osmun 1952: 6). Similarly, two watches were worn simultaneously, hanging from tassels on either side of the breeches, jangling as one walked (Quicherat 1875: 605). Fashion of course had undergone regular change for centuries; but the pace seems to have speeded up, resulting in a dizzying whirl in which seasonal change was replaced by monthly, weekly or even daily change, as clothing and silhouettes were named for events of a public and political nature.

"Macaronic" Poetry: A New Derivation?

There are other forerunners for the usage of the word macaroni that revolve around a particular construction of language. This may derive from a pun that parts of the better-educated eighteenth-century public would have enjoyed, that of the paired meanings of "noodle" and "macaronic" poetry, which was a burlesque of Latin forms, designed to be witty. Comments on both types survive in the correspondence of Walpole (Lewis 1937–83 vol. 18: 315; vol. 20: 219; vol. 16: 141). The term "macaronic" had been first used in the 1490s to describe Paduan and other Italian poetry in which Latin forms were mixed with the vernacular, the latter being given correct Latin endings. As Wenzel notes, Teofilo Folengo (d. 1544) "adopted this practice as a medium for wit, playfulness, and parody," and wrote that "macaronic poems must have nothing but fat, coarseness, and gross words in them" (Wenzel 1994: 3). The sense of burlesque and admixture, characteristic of the eighteenth-century view of the male macaroni who merged masculine and feminine personae in his appearance, as well as the English and the foreign, gave an added resonance to the term. Wenzel notes that the function of macaronic verse in Middle English was in some cases to satirize the true Latin of, for instance, the Vulgate Bible, and in others to characterize good and evil figures by the language they speak (Wenzel 1994: 4). This helps explain the relish contemporaries took in describing the male macaroni as a type of gender-hybrid. The *Oxford English Dictionary* describes macaronic as "a burlesque form of verse in which vernacular words are introduced in a Latin context with Latin terminations and in Latin constructions . . . Hence of language, style, etc.: Resembling the mixed jargon of macaronic poetry" (Wenzel 1994: 3–4). Burlesque by definition makes a mockery of both genre and stable identity, particular pre-occupations of the contemporary reaction to the macaroni. Wit was nearly always associated with the macaronic or foppish persona—sometimes through their being attacked for a complete lack thereof—and the word probably entered colloquial English through some combination of these terms in both high and popular culture. The expression continued to circulate into the nineteenth century, an anthology of macaronic poetry being published in 1831 (Sandys 1831). Latham's *Dictionary* (1870) also recorded the meaning of macaroni as "a droll or fool" (Latham 1870, vol. II, part 1: 140). Cauldrons of the food macaroni had also featured in some early European carnival parades, accompanying a fat man (Burke 1978: 185). A macaroni caricature played directly with the analogy between food and the fop: *The Salutation Tavern* (H. W. Bunbury, publisher J. Bretherton, 20 March 1773), is subtitled "Macaroni & other Soups hot every day." The term "macaroni" thus conjured meanings referring to burlesque, carnival, carousing, food, excess and satiety. A more perfect term to denote the reign of fashion could not be imagined; might "macaroni" be the most apt description for a fashion victim ever coined?

Aristocratic macaronies such as Charles James Fox were noted for their wit and urbanity, which was derived from their observations of Paris salon life, a sign of a courtly persona. The use of word-play relies on rhetoric, not reality, for hilarity; the ability of language to construct reality is celebrated. The affected speech of the macaroni circles made extensive use of French and certain pronunciations; cowcumber (cucumber), Jarsey (Jersey), charrit (chariot), gould (gold), bal-cōny (bāl-cony) and Lunnon (London) (Stirling 1911: 322). When this taste is played out in the realm of caricature, the macaronies are portrayed as full of empty speech and of no substance. The notion of the macaroni as superficial, shallow and potentially fraudulent is employed in a line of text attached to a subsidiary scene of a political caricature *c.*1774, a satire on the coin act. A man in macaroni dress accosts a courtesan, who holds out a scale and states, "You Maccaronys [*sic*] are light Chaps y^{r} Gold may be as light as yourself I'll weigh first" (George 1935: 171). In another version the macaroni has handed the harlot a guinea; she weighs it and finds it defective; he pouts (C. Bowles, *The Light Guinea, or the Blade in the Dumps*, *c.*1770). This might refer also to a defective macaroni (hetero)sexuality (McNeil 1999).

In performing the artificiality of language, the macaroni frequently exaggerated the artificiality of its actual production; his speech itself was considered unusual and affected. Macaroni talk is strewn with "mem" and snuff is often "snush." Such speech patterns and inane discussions were also associated in the eighteenth-century mind with satires on wealthy women; they can be found in a satirical account of a woman's day in *The Spectator,* 1712. Botsford quotes this passage, which is clearly satirical, as a concrete source for the typical events of a wealthy woman's day, and their "aimless existence," which it clearly is not. This type of "diary" entry was very popular in the press and was often used to satirize fashionability. Its misappropriation indicates the difficulty of treating macaroni "documents" as if they are fact, when they appear in the context of a press packed with squibs and fabricated reportage. The events and the cadence of the lady's speech here, as well as the inanity, typify satires of fashion generally and inflect later representations of macaronic behavior. Pet monkeys, lap-dogs, snuff-boxes, miniatures, self-absorption and vanity are all characteristics transferred to the macaroni, whose behavior thus had to be read as culturally feminine. *The Spectator* example reads:

> *Wednesday*. From Eight till Ten, Drank two Dishes of
> Chocolate in Bed, and fell asleep after 'em.
> From Ten to Eleven. Eat a Slice of Bread and Butter,
> drank a Dish of Bohea, read the *Spectator*.
> From Eleven to One. At my Toilet, try'd a new Head.
> Gave Orders for Veny to be combed and washed. Mem. I
> look best in Blue.
> From One till Half an Hour after Two. Drove to the
> *Change*. Cheapened a Couple of Fans.
> Till Four. At Dinner. Mem. Mr. Froth passed by in
> his new Liveries . . .
> From Four to Six. Dressed, paid a Visit to old Lady Blithe,
> and her Sister, having heard they were gone out of Town that
> Day . . .
> *Thursday* . . . Sent Frank to know how my Lady Hectick rested after
> her Monkey's leaping out at Window.
> Looked pale. Fontange tells me my Glass is not true . . .
> From Four to Eleven. Saw Company. Mr Froth's Opinion of
> Milton. His Account of the Mohocks. His Fancy
> for a Pin-Cushion. Picture in the Lid of his Snuff-Box. Old
> Lady Faddle promises me her Woman to cut my Hair . . . (Botsford
> 1924: 274–5).

When in 1786 *The Merry Andrew; or, Macaroni Jester. A Choice Collection of Funny Jokes, Merry Stories, Droll Adventures, Frolicksome Tales, Witty Quibbles, Youthful Pranks*, . . . was published, macaroni in itself must have meant something comical, for this text contains no other reference to macaronies apart from a poem in which a monkey is transformed into a Beau (*Merry Andrew* 1786: 50–1). As late as the 1930s a novel used the notion of macaroni as a type of nonsense to mock regulation (Plunkett 1934). The term "macaroni" thus enjoyed a long after-life within English popular culture.

Macaronis and Methodology

The macaroni was remembered in the nineteenth century as a colorful oddity representative of a romantic past (Chambers 1864: 31–3), until the cataloguers of the British Museum's eighteenth-century satirical prints put the study on to a more documentary footing. The macaronies are best known today through their representation in visual caricature. Dorothy George's revised catalogue of the collection lists about 150 prints that include the word "macaroni" in their title; there are many more that allude to the macaroni by their iconography or in the accompanying text (George 1935). The macaronies thus form the most substantial sub-grouping of the caricatures of manners produced in England in the 1770s. Indeed, classed as a genre the macaronies are only outnumbered by the very large body of political caricatures published in the late eighteenth century. Of this category they also form a sub-set, as political identities like Charles James Fox were widely known and caricatured as macaronies. Notably, macaroni satires are more numerous than caricatures of the absurdities of women's dress at this time, an interesting inversion of the persistent Western cultural association of females with vanity and fashion (Donald 1996: 76–8). Despite what is often said regarding the complementary nature of eighteenth-century male and female fashion, women participated differently in the fashion system even at this date. Although there is no comparable English study, Daniel Roche's analyses of French inventories indicate that noble women and female servants nearly always had larger and more valuable wardrobes than their male counterparts; the values of wardrobes of "ordinary" people were very comparable between genders (D. Roche 1994: 96–9). It is reasonable to suppose that this trend was also manifested at least as clearly in English society at large, a culture generally more suspicious of male sartorial splendor than the French. Although women's reputed propensity for excess and social emulation was derided, there was also a body of discourse that argued that ornament and adornment were natural to the female sex. Rousseau's famous pronouncement in *Emile* is paradigmatic: "Here is a little girl busy all day with her doll . . . there is no mistaking her bent . . . She is more eager for adornment than for food . . . in due time she will be her own doll" (Rousseau 1993: 396). The appearance of a sub-culture of such gaudily dressed men as the macaronies upset this cultural understanding, and accounts in part for the satirical invective directed against them.

The approach of pioneering historians of the caricature such as George Paston and M. Dorothy George was to match caricature with real events and individuals in an unproblematic manner (Paston 1905 and George

1935). Twentieth-century social history used the macaronies as mirrors of contemporary events and fixations; costume history to illustrate the excesses of fashion. A study of the macaroni can utilize a broad range of sources in order to elucidate a form of representation that functioned simultaneously as actuality and fiction. Caricature as a genre needs to be treated cautiously, so that the figure of the macaroni might emerge in a more nuanced way from the exaggerated, fantastic and comic elements of these lampooning images. Men as disparate as Sir Joseph Banks, Dr Solander, the politician Charles James Fox, the preacher William Dodd and the painter Richard Cosway were caricatured as macaronies in their day. Topical interest in the macaroni peaked in the first half of the 1770s, when descriptions and images of the macaronies were published in the principal periodicals such as *Town and Country Magazine*, *The London Magazine*, *The Universal Magazine* and *The Lady's Magazine*. A group of macaronies featured in the so-called Vauxhall Affair (1773), in which young men insulted a woman, an event that generated a great deal of periodical and newspaper discussion. The episode has been analyzed as one of Miles Ogborn's case-studies of London's eighteenth-century "geographies" of modernity. Ogborn reads the promenading macaronies at Vauxhall Gardens as emblematic of the contemporary mapping of masculinity with new spaces of consumption, fashionability and commodified leisure (Ogborn 1998: 133–42). Macaronies and their representations also spilled over in the space of the streets and the print-sellers. In 1772 *The London Magazine* noted of the macaroni: "The only thing to be said in defence of it is, that the character is harmless; it is rather foolish than vicious. As it is now at its height, our print-shops are filled with Macaronies of a variety of kinds, representing with much drollery the absurdity of this species of character in various professions" (Stephens and Hawkins 1883: 827).

Throughout 1772, *Town and Country Magazine* printed satirical letters to the editor and articles that brought the existence of the macaroni to the reader's attention. From the beginning the macaroni was posed as a hot-house exquisite who was corrupted by urban mores and in turn inflicted them on his country cousins. On return to his provincial home, this macaroni is reported to note, "Not a moment's felicity can I enjoy with such shocking wretches—hem—where's my shiff box?," a reference both to that essential accessory the snuff box and to the affected tone that became a hallmark of the macaroni (*Town and Country*, March 1772: 152). A periodical, *Macaroni and Theatrical Magazine*, capitalized on their topicality and ran in 1773. Interest extended beyond the middle-class literature represented by these journals to a song-book that included a tune on the subject of the macaroni around this time. This text was very cheaply printed and may have circulated amongst less affluent areas of the community, its rhyme perhaps drawn from a popular song or ditty ("Bottle and Friends [*sic*] Garland" *c.*1765). The tune "The Macaroni" included the following paradigmatic lines:

With little hat and hair-drest high
And whip to ride a pony,
If that you take a right survey
Denotes a Macaroni . . .

Five pounds of hair they wear behind,
The ladies to delight oh,
Their senses give unto the wind,
To make themselves a fight oh! (Anon. *c.*1765: 7).

A study of the macaroni provides an opportunity to study the slippage between the "reality" and representation of a sartorial system and the distinction between the two. Costume historians throughout the twentieth century have seized on the more piquant and amusing descriptions of macaronies that circulated in ladies' and other middle-class magazines of the early 1770s. Indeed, it is hard to resist these colorful and amusing passages, which cast light on male dress and act as a counter to the preponderance of description and information on and analysis of women's dress in the same period. Rather than deploying them simply as evidence, they can be scrutinized as fictions and representations. As certain "real" historical figures were labelled "macaronies" there is a strong temptation to discuss the phenomenon in these terms. But the term was generated, spread and expanded in popular discourse; it thus also functions as a fiction, like the *précieuses* of the seventeenth century and the *Incroyables* and *Merveilleuses* of the *Directoire*. We can only conjecture exactly what a macaroni may have looked like; this endeavour is made possible through the comparison of respectful and scurrilous representations of the same individuals who were considered macaronies. Fortunately, this can be done very easily in the cases of the politician Charles James Fox, the naturalist Sir Joseph Banks and the artist Richard Cosway, and yields different results and issues related to class and political affiliation in each case. The macaroni case thus highlights how different types of visual "evidence" might be mobilized in costume history.

The social politics of the macaronies is complex. Many of the first macaronies were extremely wealthy, but the most famous of all, Charles James Fox, did not side with the Court, and came from a Francophile and Jacobite background, later becoming a radical Whig. Others such as the painter Richard Cosway and the court preacher the Reverend Dodd were court followers, sycophantic in their dress and their motives. Macaroni caricatures of Julius "Soubise," the "Mungo" macaroni, parodied a foppish upstart whose outfits and entertainments, financed by the Duchess of Queensbury, affronted both racial and social expectations of an African male. The court was peripatetic, moving between St James's, Kensington, Hampton Court and Windsor. Yet the macaronies kept court dress in the streets whether the Royal family was in residence or not. Like gambling debts, dress was a very visible part of conspicuous consumption.

A lavish dress, like the sumptuous Whig country estates and town-houses (Spencer House was built in the 1760s) indicated that here was the true power in England. As the Whigs' forebears had opposed absolutism, there was an irony in this re-importation of French court dress, wit and manners as a style detached from its original premise. The young Whigs wore aristocratic dress without the autocratic agenda inherent in the French original. The French had standardized dress and manners as a hegemonic gesture; re-imported into England they had new meanings. Fox loved Paris and her society but hated the Bourbon autocracy (Derry 1972: 295). Thus his adoption of macaroni dress was not a tribute to monarchy but a statement of a cosmopolitan outlook and Whig confidence. Fox himself does not appear to have used the term "macaroni" to describe himself but preferred the term *petit-maître*, a term that was negative in the hands of a *philosophe*, but affectionate within salon society. In a letter to his father requesting that he stay on at Eton he half-jokingly suggested, "the *petit maître de Paris* is converted into an Oxford pedant" (Mitchell 1992: 9).

The macaroni sources often employ the notion of John Bull's being affronted and unseated by the "new" male fashionability. This reflects less the idea that an interest in fashion on the part of men was new, than the notion that more men were being fashionable. The overall impression of the caricatures is that both sexes were becoming more infected with the "vice of fashion," a fact that has been confirmed in English and French socio-economic research into the nature of eighteenth-century consumption (McKendrick, Brewer and Plumb 1982; Brewer, Porter, Staves and Bermingham 1993; Roche 1994; Vickery 1998; Weatherill 1991 and 1996). If some members of the lower orders emulated macaroni dress, as sources suggest, then the question of motive becomes even more complicated. That social inferiors might ape the dress of their betters indicates that the pre-modern pattern of a hierarchical dress system underpinned by sumptuary law had completely collapsed. As Ogborn argues in his analysis of eighteenth-century pleasure-garden culture, fashionable male dress was played out "within the streets of a commercial city and nation rather than among the ornate displays of the Renaissance court" (Ogborn 1998: 138). Commenting upon this shift, *Universal Magazine* noted of the macaronies: "was it not for an awkwardness in the gait, a clownishness of manners, and a solecism in speech, the Gentlemen of birth and fortune would not be known from him" (*Universal Magazine* 1772: 209). This is a charge that was more commonly directed at women, particularly merchants' wives and courtesans who could afford fine clothing; but it also extended to servants. Cheaper copies of dress and fabric types previously reserved for the nobility, and increased disposable incomes for the middle classes, complicated the visual imagery of dress in England.

As Barker-Benfield notes, fashion demanded display as well as purchase (Barker-Benfield 1992: 176). The culture of display was no longer limited to the higher echelons of court society but was spreading rapidly into other ranks and urban spaces. This was partly encouraged by the necessity for the aristocracy and the gentry to integrate socially, and marry for financial reasons, the *raison d'être* of the establishment of the resort town of Bath, at which macaronic behavior flourished in the 1760s and 1770s (Varey 1990: 101–2). Mrs Montagu complained of Bath "Misses who strut about in morning in Riding dresses and uniforms and the Maccaronis [*sic*] who trip in pumps and with Parasols over their heads . . ." (Buck 1979: 100). Bath was a stage for the display of clothing and manners, more or less fine, as the daughters of merchants tried to tempt those less wealthy but more titled than themselves. As the old money and the *nouveaux riches* arrived for the season, so too did the purveyors of luxury and the appearance trades, as Daniel Roche so aptly calls them. Their own appearances were walking advertisements for fashions of excess. Bath had its own print-shops in which the latest engravings were displayed (Fawcett 1990: 62); the town itself was fertile ground for the satirist. The Darlys played up these associations, producing several images of Bath macaronies. *The Emaciated Bath Macaroni* (George 1935: cat. no. 5032) depicted one of the invalids of Bath, whose dress was as grotesque as his gouty body; *The Bath Macaroni* shows an elegant man with exaggerated wig-bag and hanger (dress-sword). Christopher Anstey was amongst those who penned hilarious satires upon the Bath macaroni, and H. Bunbury produced drawings for caricatures of Bath macaronies and fashionability (Anstey 1994 and 1997).

Those above the level of the laboring poor, such as artisans and servants, also had access to genuine and copied articles of the types of clothing previously reserved for the gentry and aristocracy, and wore them in a jaunty and insouciant manner that complicated the sartorial hierarchy, and enraged social conservatives. As well as including clothing as part of wages it was common to leave clothing in a will; Horace Walpole left his whole wardrobe to his servant (Lewis 1937–83 vol. 30: 360). The poem *Time Was* in *Town Ecologues*, by C. Jenner (1773) mocked the pretension of those who follow the dress and manners of their betters by indulging in the pursuit of fashion and leisure:

> AVARO.
> Time was, when satin waistcoats and scratch wigs,
> Enough distinguish'd all the city prigs,
> Whilst ev'ry sunshine Sunday saw them run
> To club their sixpences at *Islington*;
> When graver citizens, in suits of brown,
> Lin'd ev'ry dusty avenue to town,
> Or led the children and the loving spouse,
> To spend two shillings at *White Conduit House*:
> But now, the 'prentices, in suits of green,
> At *Richmond* or at *Windsor* may be seen;
> Where in mad parties they run down to dine

To play at gentlefolks, and drink bad wine . . .
PRUDENTIO.
'Tis true my friend; and thus throughout the nation
Prevails the general love of dissipation:
It matters little where their sports begin,
Whether at *Arthur's*, or the *Bowl and Pin*;
Whether they tread the gay *Pantheon*'s round,
Or play at skittles at *St Giles'* pound,
The self-same idle spirit drags them on,
and peer and porter are alike undone:
Whilst thoughtless imitation leads the way
And laughs at all the grave and wise can say (George 1928: 166–7).

The reference to "children and the loving spouse" denotes the emergent bourgeois family; "Avaro," The Miser, "Prudentio", Prudence, the enemy of excess; green was the popular macaroni color. "Thoughtless imitation" mocks the "grave and wise," suggesting also death and Judgement of "true" character. A nineteenth-century periodical recorded a similar theme in a song entitled *The Macaroni,* set to the air "Nancy Dawson," which may reflect a lost eighteenth-century tune. In the case of the macaroni such popular sources are part of the archaeology of popular culture and attitudes, otherwise almost impossible to retrieve:

. . . The cits that used, like Jerry Sneak,
To dress and walk out once a week,
And durst not to their betters speak,
Are all grown jolly crony;
Each sneak is now a buckish blade,
When in the Park, but talk of trade,
He thinks you mean him to degrade—
Each cit's a macaroni (Chambers 1864: 32).

As well as those in service, the sector involved with the appearance industries was large. E. P. Thompson notes a growing confidence amongst some workers, and observes:

> the enlargement of that sector of the economy which was independent of a client relationship to the gentry. The "subject" economy remained huge: not only the direct retainers of the great house . . . but the further concentric rings of economic clientship—the equestrian trades and luxury trades . . . But the century saw a growing area of independence within which the small employers and labourers felt their client relationship to the gentry very little or not at all (Thompson 1993: 39).

These "employers and labourers" included clothing workers and urban artisans who had access to fashionable goods, who "escaped from the social controls of the manorial village and were not yet subject to the discipline of factory labor" (Thompson 1993: 40). Their growing confidence might be expressed sartorially. Although information about this group is more limited, it is possible that some of them adopted a macaronic persona, particularly in urban areas. Many artisans were of course prosperous themselves; the famous cabinet-maker John Cobb, contemporary with the macaronies, was later described as a "singularly haugty [*sic*] character . . . one of the proudest men in England . . . he always appeared in full dress of the most superb and costly kind, in which state he would strut through his workshop giving orders to his men" (Jackson-Stops 1985: 328). The press was full of complaints of men of "mean station" getting their hands on superior fashions and making macaronies of themselves, the exhibition of "abominable vanity in the little" (*Universal Magazine* 1772: 209). *Macaroni Scavoir* [sic] *Vivre Magazine* reported upon a masquerade at Carlisle house at which "a maccaroni [*sic*] tallow chandler, and another of the same trade with his basket, as greasy as the best of them" were present (*Macaroni, Scavoir* [sic] *Vivre, and Theatrical Magazine*, February 1774: 205). The grease of the tallow trade alludes here variously to a slickness of manners and the social stain that association with such types might leave behind, as well as to the grease of the cheap or rancid wig. The new macaroni hair-styles spread quickly to less affluent youth. Sir Joshua Reynolds' young provincial nephew, Samuel Johnson (b. 1754), convinced by friends to visit an Assembly at Islington (1775), was lent lace ruffles and "They persuaded me to wear a bag and a sword, but I found myself not singular in a twisted tail" (Radcliffe 1930: 92–3). He must have become accustomed to the style, for in a letter that year to his dismayed mother, who was horrified at the thought of her son's Devonshire curls being plaited and dressed, he wrote:

> This is in defence of my tail, which I must wear in London where none but clergymen and boys wear their hair untied; the place only makes the difference; a tail here is the same as curls in the country, and silk stockings the same as worsted; but if it is only for my hair and not for my head that you are concern'd I can assure you that it is in better order than it has been for months . . . (Radcliffe 1930: 96).

As this young man had to leave London each weekend for lack of a decent suit (Radcliffe 1930: 119) this indicates that elements such as the hair-style were sufficient to mark one out as a macaroni. Although Walpole referred generally to the high-born in his discussion of the macaroni, in an intriguing letter of 1775 he provided a rare insight into the persona of another non-noble macaroni. He discusses the death of "One of our Maccaronis," "Captain Mawhood, the tea-man's son" (Lewis 1937–83 vol. 39: 250). Lewis identified the Captain as James Mawhood (died 1775), brigadier and lieutenant, and the son of a tea-merchant in the New Exchange (Lewis 1937–83 vol. 39: 250, notes 7–8). Mawhood is a tantalizing reminder that not all men of fashion were high-born ; Walpole notes that Mawhood was mocked as Captain "Hyson" (a green tea) by his fellow officers—green recurring as a color favored by the macaroni, possibly because traditionally it was a more technically difficult and expensive color. As the print industry and the popular press indicate, a macaroni persona spread into the general population with different effects and results.

As caricatures went up in print-shop windows, and macaroni figures appeared on the boards in Drury Lane, viewers may have found these images to be riotous critiques of the nobility in general. Thompson's masterful study of "the view from below" indicates that the "lower orders" in England did not simply accept the aristocracy in wondrous admiration, but had been involved for generations in activities that ranged from gentle mocking to urban terrorism: "There is a sense in which rulers and crowd needed each other, watched each other, performed theatre and countertheatre to each other's auditorium, moderated each other's political behavior. This is a more active and reciprocal relationship than the one normally brought to mind under the formula 'paternalism and deference'" (Thompson 1993: 57). Thompson's study sounds a warning to the historian of the eighteenth century, and should be carefully observed in costume history: "No-one is more susceptible to the charms of the gentry's life than the historian of the eighteenth century. His major sources are in the archives of the gentry or aristocracy . . . The 'laboring poor' did not leave their workhouses stashed with documents for historians to work over nor do they invite identification with their back-breaking toil" (Thompson 1993: 17–18). The macaroni figure and the macaroni caricature may have achieved such currency because they were the perfect vehicle for Thompson's notion of the "countertheatre of the poor" (Thompson 1993: 67). As the lower orders gazed at macaroni caricatures displayed in print-shop windows and pasted up in taverns and latrines, or watched such figures tread the boards, they could not have failed to make the connection with the toffs around them. The sins of an idle aristocracy or court elite were set out in an engraving from M. Darly's second macaroni suite, *Venison & Claret, or Sr Hump^y Haunch Bar^t of Glutton Hall*, in which an obese nobleman struts along the street in the latest fashionable hair-style and suit trimmed with galloon.

Harassment and jesting were a part of life for over-dressed gentlemen who ventured into hostile territory. Reports survive of over-dressed *émigrés* in London being continually harassed for their hairstyles in the early 1790s (Chrisman 1997: 5–6). The theater of sartorial display is made all the more interesting as young male workers in the appearance industries—tailors, peruke-makers, hairdressers—adopted elements of the dress as walking advertisements for the trade in court dress upon which

their livelihoods depended. Although it is tempting to suggest that members of the appearance industries always attempted to wear lavish clothes, this probably depends upon the place and the trade. Lou Taylor, in her useful review of Harvey's *Men in Black*, notes that research by Lesley Miller on the wardrobes of Lyons silk designers indicates that their dress "was muted, based upon the 'classic' colours and fabrics deemed appropriate for the middling ranks of society . . . The little black (or grey or brown) suit was both utilitarian and self-consciously low-key, suitable for a job in which personal contacts with rich clients made competitive, showy dressing inadvisable" (Taylor 1996: 302). As Miller refers to designers, different findings might be made for the wardrobes of high-fashion purveyors, particularly in Paris. Were they always respectful, or did elements of parody emerge? Were they considered sycophants by other workers, or did they laugh at the sight of these "apes" and "monkeys," to use the standard terms that mocked fashionable pretension?

Garments as Evidence

Surviving examples of male dress that correspond to the "macaroni" description indicate the splendor and sensual appeal of such garments. Most museum costume collections that include eighteenth-century menswear hold garments related to the contemporary descriptions of macaroni dressing. This is not surprising, as these are the types of lavish garments retained and collected in the nineteenth and early-twentieth centuries as technical and aesthetic exemplars of textile design. There is difficulty in extricating or distinguishing surviving examples of "court dress" from "macaroni" dress, a very real problem considering the lack of *provenance* in this period. Elsewhere I have described holdings relevant to macaroni dress held at the Royal Ontario Museum, most of which were collected in the early years of the twentieth century (McNeil 2000). These include an English apple-green silk suit finely embroidered with swags of pink flowers and tassels, the favored macaroni color scheme cited previously (Figures 1–3), and a spectacular French gold silk lampas waistcoat, with pink and green brocading and silver sequins (Figures 4–5).

Macaroni dress-swords survive in collections including that of the British Museum. The swords were decorated with large tassels or rosettes; an elaborate pair of embroidered and painted sword-knots, English, *c.*1770, with a design of cornflowers and daisies, hand-painted and outlined in chain stitch in silver and gold, edged with *passementerie* lace, is held at Spencer House, London. Sword-knots held an erotic charge and a reference to potency; they were often worked by ladies for their gentlemen. In France the noble bride at her wedding gave gifts of expensive sword-knots for men, and fans for ladies (Chaussinand-Nogaret 1985: 120). The dress-sword also held an erotic charge, in France at least; in Baudouin's *Le Carquois épuisé* (engraving by N. de Launay, *c.*1771), a

Figure 1
Coat and waistcoat, English, green silk, embroidered, 1770s. Royal Ontario Museum 924.16.60A-B. Photo Brian Boyle, reproduced courtesy of Veronika Gervers Research Fellowship.

Figure 2
Coat, English, green silk, embroidered, 1770s. Royal Ontario Museum 924.16.60A. Photo Brian Boyle, reproduced courtesy of Veronika Gervers Research Fellowship.

dress-sword with attached ribbons lies discarded on the floor, the sign of sexual contact (d'Allemagne 1928: vol. 1, pl. CCCIV). Like the dress-sword, the over-sized macaroni sword-knot may function as a joke, as many macaronies were in fact considered defective in the matter of virility. Other macaroni accessories include the snuff-boxes and cane-handles of precious and semi-precious materials that survive in the decorative arts collections of most European museums, the glamor of which can be gauged from the relevant plates in Diderot's *Encyclopédie* (1762). The British Museum holds a sumptuous male *châtelaine à breloquet* of green enamel and gold, from which a watch is suspended (Figure 6). This object, which was hooked over the belt, often with a *fausse montre* (false watch) at one end, is the type of extravagant object associated with the macaroni stereotype. In England this fashionable manner of wearing a watch was passing from the male into the female wardrobe by the late 1780s (Tait 1984: 86).

Corsages or 'nosegays' also recur in macaroni caricatures; they were part of aristocratic male attire in the eighteenth century, but the subtle messages were in the styling. The key to the macaroni was excess. Walpole

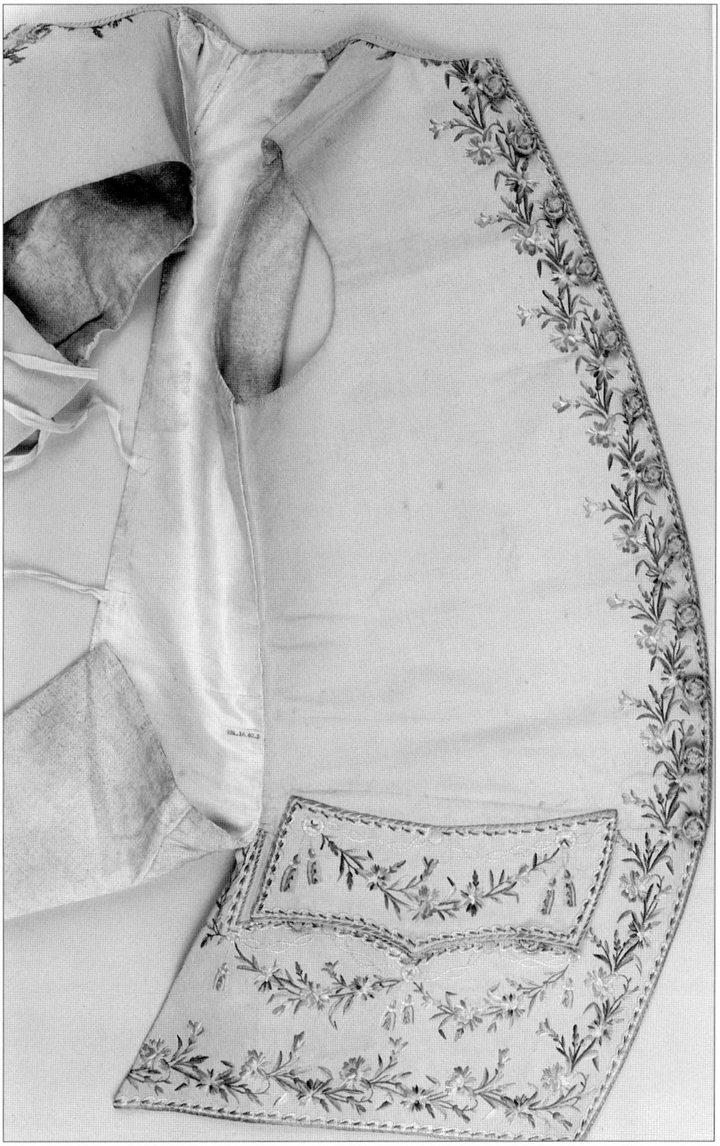

Figure 3
Waistcoat, English, green silk, embroidered, detail of pocket, 1770s. Royal Ontario Museum 924.16.60B. Photo Brian Boyle, reproduced courtesy of Veronika Gervers Research Fellowship.

characterized the macaronies as sporting massive nosegays or corsages: "Lord Nuneham's garden is the quintessence of nosegays: I wonder some macaroni does not offer ten thousand pounds for it—but indeed the flowers come in their natural season, and take care to bring their perfumes along with them" (Lewis 1937–83 vol. 28: 105). These probably resembled the style of the substantial corsages worn at the French court, illustrated in Jean-Michel Moreau le Jeune's drawings for Nicolas-Edmé Restif (Rétif) de la Bretonne's *Monument du Costume Physique et Moral de la Fin du Dix-huitième Siècle* (several series and editions, 1775–1789), which depict a nobleman's *toilette*.

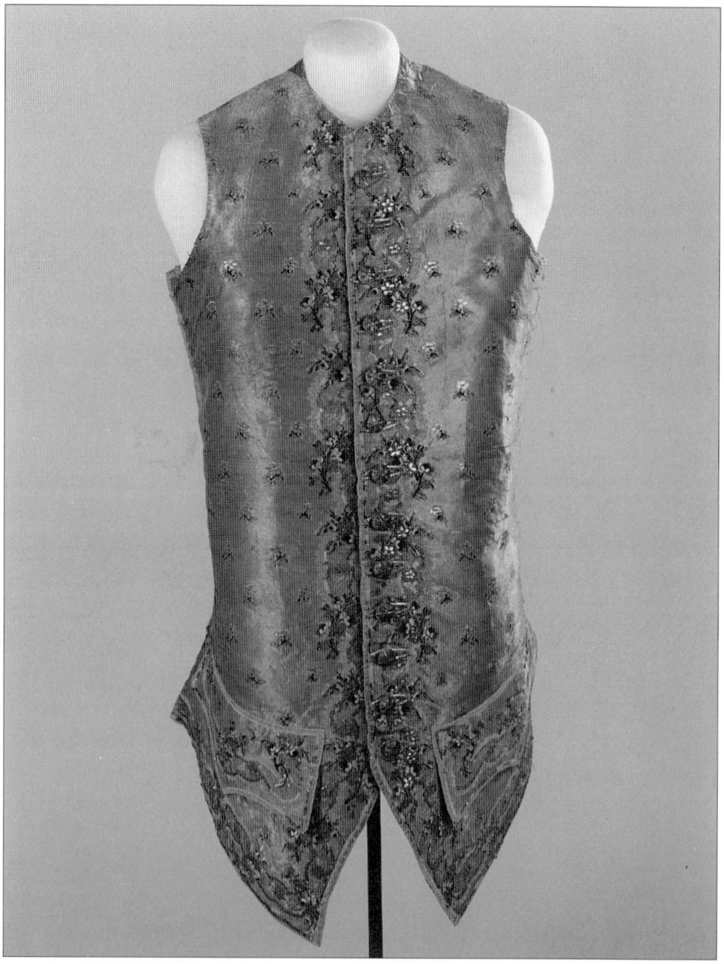

Figure 4
Waistcoat, French, gold silk lampas, brocaded, embroidered, tabby ground; winding band brocaded in pink silk and silver *frisé* with floral sprays brocaded in colored silks and chenilles and embroidered with silver *filé*, sequins and coils of silver wire; buttons embroidered with silver *lamé* and *filé*, *c*.1760. Royal Ontario Museum 920.28.10. Photo Brian Boyle, reproduced courtesy of Veronika Gervers Research Fellowship.

Figure 5
Waistcoat, French, detail of center front, *c.*1760. Royal Ontario Museum 920.28.10. Photo Brian Boyle, reproduced courtesy of Veronika Gervers Research Fellowship.

Conclusion

The macaroni contradicted the notion that masculine clothing expressed a stable, continuous and inherent self, overturning pre-modern dress hierarchies. Rather, he posited a self that exists only in performance, brought into being by such performative factors as gesture, speech and dress. The macaroni cannot therefore be fully understood simply by analyzing the clothes he wore, deposited as surviving samples in the world's museums. In the same manner, the text of a play languishing unrealized on stage, or in studies that do not refer to performance productions, is diminished in its meaning. Nevertheless, just as much can be deduced from the text of a play, analysis of surviving macaroni costume exposes the visual flux such clothing brought to the spaces of a city such as London, redefining it as a modern center of international trade and commodity culture. While an emphasis on performance means the constructed histories of the individual wearers of macaroni clothing must be analyzed, it is as records of performance that their lasting depictions in

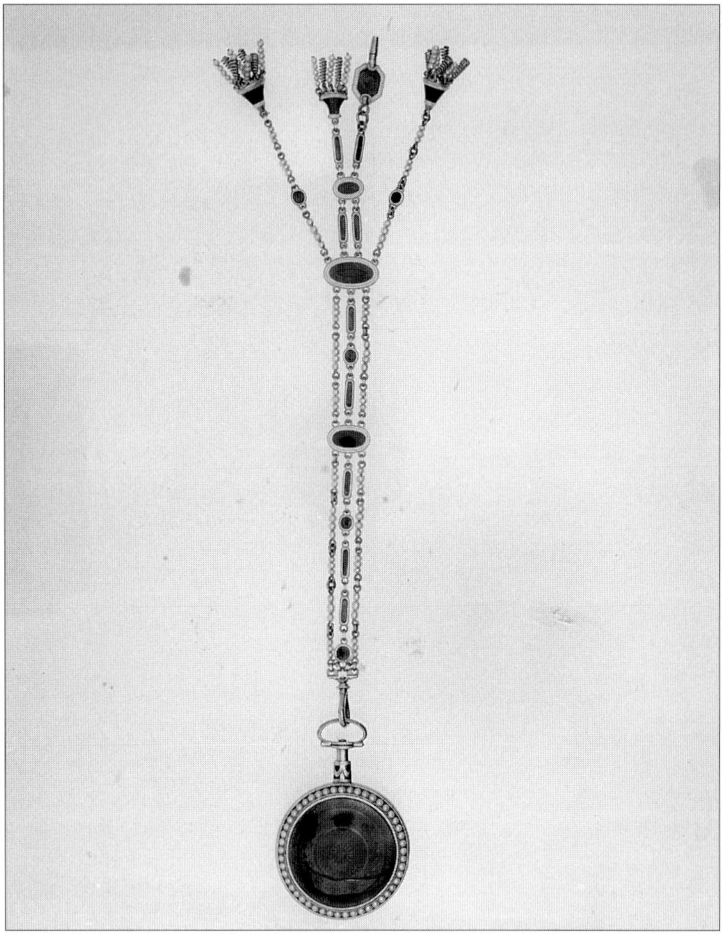

Figure 6
Enamel and gold 'macaroni' chatelaine, late-18th century, retailed by Richard Clarke & Son, London. British Museum. MLA 1905, 2-10. 1 (rear view). Copyright The British Museum.

text and image must be read, not as some stable identifier of what their characters were "actually" like. Any meeting of macaronies could be the "macaroni club"; it was more a process than a real place. A macaroni need not be a gilded Whig enjoying club-land, but could be a male of any order adopting some element of the macaroni persona. This spread of fashionability accounts for part of the contemporary fascination with the macaroni figure. Men who dressed above their station in ultra-fashionable modes were subjected to a triple mockery, that of transgressions of status, gender and sexuality. They could be viewed as upstarts asserting a social status above their "true" station. They could be pilloried as effeminate and invoke anxieties about a blurring of gender distinction. They could pejoratively be identified, or possibly even identify themselves, as sodomites (McNeil 1999). The macaroni also disrupted stable notions of racial identity at a time when these were being deployed in the interests of British social cohesion, with his exaggerated Francophile performance. He exposed Englishness, too, as a performance.

To analyze the macaronies is nothing less than to ask, what is fashion? The answer may be that fashion is no "thing" at all, but a process, an endless series of reflections between image and reality. A "real" macaroni saw exaggerated images of "himself" on stage, in the print-shops and on the streets, and emulated them; perhaps seeking to outdo the image in his own reality. Caricature actually helped create the identity, its derision making a space for a resistant subjectivity. This may be something fundamental to the development of subcultures; in taking an image of ridicule and exaggerating it an identity was formulated. The deconstruction of the dichotomies of image/wearer, clothing/human in the real and unreal figure of the macaroni is the key to the conflation of this character with "fashion." For a few years in the late eighteenth century the macaroni was nothing less than modern fashion itself. It is the power of fashion as modern commodity that invoked the anxieties that saw the macaroni simultaneously mocked and celebrated in public discourse and popular culture.

Notes

1. This article is drawn from my Ph.D. thesis, "Fashion Victims: Class, Gender, Sexuality and the Macaroni, *c.*1765–80," Department of Art History and Theory, University of Sydney, 1999. I would like to acknowledge the very helpful comments of readers including Dr. Christopher Breward, Dr. Michael Carter, Mr. Ian Henderson, Dr. Jennifer Milam, Dr. Gillian Russell and Dr. Valerie Steele, and the anonymous readers at *Fashion Theory*. Ms. Kay Spilker assisted at the Los Angeles County Museum, as did Ms. Anu Liivandi, Ms. Shannon Elliott and Dr. Alexandra Palmer at the Royal Ontario Museum, Toronto. Mr. David Thompson, Curator of Horology, and Ms. Judy Rudoe, Assistant Keeper, Department of Medieval and Later Antiquities, provided assistance at the British Museum. Parts of the research were conducted with the assistance of the Veronika Gervers Research Fellowship in Textiles and Costume History, Royal Ontario Museum.
2. At one point Lewis claimed that the macaroni club was located in King Street, St James's Square (Lewis 1937–83 vol. 38: 306, Note 6). In a later note Lewis admitted that the reference to the club was probably a newspaper squib (Lewis 1937–83 vol. 10: 139, Note 11).
3. "Capes" refers here to collars; a turned-down collar, however narrow, was called a cape: C. Willett and Phillis Cunnington. 1972. *Handbook of English Costume in the Eighteenth Century* (Boston: Plays Inc.), p.38.

References

Allemagne, Henry René d'. 1928. *Les Accessoires du Costume et du Mobilier, depuis le treizième jusqu'au milieu du dixneuvième siècle*, 3 vols. Paris: Schemit.

Allen, Robert J. 1967. *The Clubs of Augustan London*. Hamden, CT: Archon.

Anon. n.d. [*c*.1765]. *The Bottle and Friends [sic] Garland, containing Four Excellent New Songs . . . V. The Macaroni*. No publisher.

Anstey, Christopher. 1994 [1766]. *The New Bath Guide*, Introduction and notes by Gavin Turner. Bristol: Broadcast Books.

——. 1997 [1776]. *An Election Ball*, Introduction and notes by Gavin Turner. Bristol: Broadcast Books.

Ayling, Stanley. 1991. *Fox. The Life of Charles James Fox*. London: John Murray.

Barker-Benfield, G. J. 1992. *The Culture of Sensibility. Sex and Society in Eighteenth-Century Britain*. Chicago and London: University of Chicago Press.

Berry, Christopher J. 1994. *The Idea of Luxury. A Conceptual and Historical Investigation*. Cambridge: Cambridge University Press.

Botsford, Jay Barrett. 1924. *English Society in the Eighteenth Century as influenced from oversea* [sic]. New York: Macmillan Company.

Brewer, J., R. Porter, S. Staves and A. Bermingham (eds). 1993. *Consumption and the World of Goods*. London: Routledge.

Buck, Anne. 1979. *Dress in Eighteenth-Century England*. New York: Holmes and Meier.

Burke, Peter. 1978. *Popular Culture in Early Modern Europe*. London: Temple Smith.

Chambers, R. (ed.). 1864. The *Book of Days. A Miscellany of Popular Antiquities in connection with the Calendar, including anecdote, biography, and history, curiosities of literature and oddities of human life and character*, Vol. II, 7 July.

Chancellor, E. Beresford. n.d. [1920]. *The XVIIIth Century in London. An Account of its Social Life and Arts*. London: B. T. Batsford.

Chaussinand-Nogaret, Guy. 1985. *The French Nobility in the Eighteenth Century. From Feudalism to Enlightenment*, trans. William Doyle. Cambridge: Cambridge University Press.

Chrisman, Kimberly. 1997. "*L'émigration à la mode*. Clothing worn and produced by the French émigré community in England from the Revolution to the Restoration." MA Thesis. The Courtauld Institute of Art.

Derry, John W. 1972. *Charles James Fox*. London: B. T. Batsford.

Donald, Diana. 1996. *The Age of Caricature. Satirical Prints in the Reign of George III*. New Haven, CT and London: Yale University Press.

Egan, Pierce. 1823 (revised edn. of work published 1785). *Grose's Classical Dictionary of the Vulgar Tongue, revised and corrected, with*

the addition of numerous slang phrases, collected from tried authorities. London: for the Editor.
Fawcett, Trevor. 1990. "Eighteenth-Century Shops and the Luxury Trade." *Bath History*, II: 49–75.
George, Mary Dorothy. 1928. *England in Johnson's Day*. London: Methuen and Co.
——. 1935. *Catalogue of Political and Personal Satires Preserved in the Department of Prints and Drawings in the British Museum*, Vol. V, 1771–1783. London: Trustees of the British Museum.
Jackson-Stops, Gervase (ed.). 1985. *The Treasure Houses of Britain. Five Hundred Years of Private Patronage and Art Collecting*. New Haven, CT and London: National Gallery of Art, Washington and Yale University Press.
Latham, Robert Gordon. 1870. *A Dictionary of the English Language . . .* 2 vols. London.
Lesley, Everett P., Jr. and William Osmun. 1952. *Conspicuous Waist. Waistcoats and Waistcoat Designs 1700–1952* (exhibition catalog). New York: The Cooper Union Museum for the Arts of Decoration.
Lewis, Wilmarth S. (ed.). 1937–83. *The Yale Edition of Horace Walpole's Correspondence*. 48 vols. New Haven, CT and London: Yale University Press.
*The Macaroni, Scavoir [*sic*] Vivre, and Theatrical Magazine*, October 1773–October 1774.
McKendrick, Neil, John Brewer and J. H. Plumb. 1982. *The Birth of a Consumer Society. The Commercialization of Eighteenth-Century England*. Bloomington, IN: Indiana University Press.
McNeil, Peter. 1999. " 'That Doubtful Gender': Macaroni Dress and Male Sexualities." *Fashion Theory*, 3(4): 411–47.
——. 2000. "Fashion Victims: Macaroni Dress at the ROM." *Rotunda. The Magazine of the Royal Ontario Museum*, 32(3): 36–42.
The Merry Andrew; or, Macaroni Jester. A Choice Collection of Funny Jokes, Merry Stories, Droll Adventures, Frolicksome Tales, Witty Quibbles, Youthful Pranks, . . . 1786. London: No publisher.
Mitchell, Leslie George. 1992. *Charles James Fox*. Oxford: Oxford University Press.
Musée de la Mode et du Costume. 1983. *Indispensables Accessoires XVIe–XXe siècle* (exhibition catalog). Paris: Musée de la Mode et du Costume.
Ogborn, Miles. 1998. *Spaces of Modernity. London Geographies, 1680–1780*. New York and London: Guilford Press.
Paston, George. 1905. *Social Caricature in the Eighteenth Century*. London: Methuen and Co.
[Plunkett, C.] Lord Dunsany [pseudonym]. 1934. *If I were Dictator. The Pronouncements of the Grand Macaroni*. London: Methuen.
Pointon, Marcia. 1993. *Hanging the Head. Portraiture and Social Formation in Eighteenth-Century England*. New Haven, CT and London: Yale University Press.

Quicherat, J. 1875. *Histoire du Costume en France depuis les temps les plus reculés jusqu'à la fin du XVIIIe siècle*. Paris: Hachette.

Radcliffe, Susan M. (ed.). 1930. *Sir Joshua's Nephew. Being Letters written, 1769–1778, by a Young Man to his Sisters*. London: John Murray.

Roche, Daniel. 1994. *The Culture of Clothing. Dress and Fashion in the "Ancien régime,"* trans. Jean Birrell. Cambridge: Cambridge University Press.

Roche, Sophie V. La. 1933. *Sophie in London, 1786. Being the Diary of Sophie V. La Roche*, trans. Clare Williams. London: Jonathan Cape.

Rousseau, Jean-Jacques. 1993 (first edn. France 1762). *Emile*, trans. Barbara Foxley. London: J. M. Dent.

[Sandys, W. (ed.)]. 1831. *Specimens of Macaronic Poetry*. London: Richard Beckley.

Siegfried, Susan L. 1995. *The Art of Louis-Léopold Boilly: Modern Life in Napoleonic France*. New Haven, CT: Yale University Press.

Stephens, Frederick George and Edward Hawkins. 1883. *Catalogue of Prints and Drawings in the British Museum. Division I. Political and Personal Satires*, Vol. 4, A.D. 1761–c. A.D. 1770. London: Trustees of the British Museum.

Stirling, A. M. W. 1911. *Annals of a Yorkshire House from the Papers of a Macaroni & his Kindred*, 2 vols. London: John Lane.

Stone, George Winchester, Jr. and George M. Kahrl. 1979. *David Garrick. A Critical Biography*. Carbondale and Edwardsville, IL: Southern Illinois University Press.

Tait, Hugh (ed.). 1984. *The Art of the Jeweller*. London: British Museum.

Taylor, Lou. 1996. "John Harvey, *Men in Black*, London, Reaktion Books, 1995" (review). *Journal of Design History* 9(4): 301–3.

Thomas, David (ed.). 1989. *Theatre in Europe: A Documentary History. Restoration and Georgian England, 1660–1788*. Cambridge: Cambridge University Press.

Thompson, E. P. 1993. *Customs in Common*. London: Penguin.

Tillyard, Stella. 1994. *Aristocrats. Caroline, Emily, Louisa, and Sarah Lennox 1740–1832*. New York: Farrar, Straus and Giroux.

Town and Country Magazine. 1772.

Toynbee, Paget (ed.). 1926. *Satirical Poems Published anonymously by William Mason with Notes by Horace Walpole, now first printed from his manuscript*. Oxford: Clarendon Press.

Trevelyan, George Otto. 1880. *The Early History of Charles James Fox*. London: Longman, Green, and Co.

Universal Magazine of Knowledge and Pleasure. October 1772.

Varey, Simon. 1990. *Space and the Eighteenth-Century English Novel*. Cambridge: Cambridge University Press.

Vickery, Amanda. 1998. *The Gentleman's Daughter. Women's Lives in Georgian England*. New Haven, CT and London: Yale University Press.

Walpole, B. C. 1806. *Recollections of the Life of the Late Right Honorable Charles James Fox; exhibiting a faithful account of the most remarkable events of his political career, and a delineation of his character as a statesman, senator, and man of fashion . . .* London: James Cundee.

Weatherill, Lorna. 1991. "Consumer Behaviour, Textiles and Dress in the Late Seventeenth and Early Eighteenth Centuries." *Textile History* 22/2: 297–310.

——. 1996. *Consumer Behaviour and Material Culture in Britain 1660–1760*, 2nd edn. London and New York: Routledge.

Wenzel, Siegfried. 1994. *Macaronic Sermons. Bilingualism and Preaching in Late-Medieval England*. Ann Arbor, MI: University of Michigan Press.

Fashion Theory, Volume 4, Issue 4, pp.405–426
Reprints available directly from the Publishers.
Photocopying permitted by licence only.

Fashioning the Gentleman: A Study of Henry Poole and Co., Savile Row Tailors 1861–1900

Fiona Anderson

Fiona Anderson is a freelance curator and lecturer who has worked at the Design Museum, the Victoria and Albert Museum and as Curator of the Conran Foundation Collection. She has taught Fashion, Textile and Design History at a range of institutions including Brighton University and the Royal College of Art.

The visual language of nineteenth-century English aristocratic life, as typified by Savile Row tailoring, has retained a cultural potency and commercial appeal to the present day, despite an almost total collapse of the social, economic and cultural formation from which it arose. The lack of published historical information available to explain this scenario inspired this research, which is based on my case-study of "Henry Poole and Co., Savile Row Tailors 1861–1900" (1998) and on the company's archives, now housed at their premises at 15 Savile Row.[1]

This article will look at the relationship between shifts in the composition and lifestyle of the late nineteenth-century wealth, social and power elite and the development of male fashion practices in that period.

It will argue that what the social historian David Cannadine refers to as the "glamour" of the English aristocracy held such an appeal as to survive the period of their decline (Cannadine 1996: 2). Elite lifestyles and the clothing associated with them were, however, reformulated by the turn of the century, owing to the broadening of "society," the influence of wealthy newcomers and changes within the aristocracy itself. This examination will further enable an assessment of the links between class, national identity, masculinities and the broader development of male fashionable identities within an urban context.

The dress of socially elite men in the late nineteenth-century has received scant academic attention to date. In contrast to eighteenth- and twentieth-century dress, it is represented in museum collections in only a minor and partial fashion. In addition, while the higher social orders are well represented in portraiture, the almost exclusive adornment of the sitters in formal dress has rendered invisible a large proportion of the elite male wardrobe. This invisibility has contributed to the wholesale acceptance of the psychologist J. C. Flugel's theory of the "Great Masculine Renunciation," which he expounded in his 1930 text *The Psychology of Clothes* as follows:

> Men may be said to have suffered a great defeat in the sudden reduction of male sartorial decorativeness which took place at the end of the eighteenth century. At about that time there occurred one of the most remarkable events in the whole history of dress, one under the influence of which we are still living, one, moreover, which has attracted far less attention than it deserves: men gave up their right to all the brighter, gayer, more elaborate, and more varied forms of ornamentation, leaving these entirely to the use of women, and thereby making their own tailoring the most austere and ascetic of the arts. Sartorially, this event has surely the right to be considered as "The Great Masculine Renunciation." Man abandoned his claim to be considered beautiful. He henceforth aimed at being only useful. So far as clothes remained of importance to him, his utmost endeavors could lie only in the direction of being "correctly" attired, not of being elegantly or elaborately attired (Flugel 1930).

These ideas have recently been challenged in a most convincing manner by Christopher Breward in his text *The Hidden Consumer: Masculinities, Fashion and City Life 1860–1914*, primarily with reference to working-class and lower-middle-class men in London (Breward 1999). This article will extend these debates by focusing on men of the class identified by Thorstein Veblen in 1899 as the "leisure class," through an examination of the business activities of a leading Savile Row tailor and the clothing consumption strategies of their customers. Although the findings are based on a limited sample, the scale of the business of Henry Poole and Co.

(who produced an average of 12,000 bespoke garments a year in the period studied) and the nature of their clientele mean that their archives provide a meaningful indication of elite clothing practices in the late nineteenth century. The article draws on a computer database that was created on the basis of a sample of the firm's 1861 and 1900 sales ledgers.[2] Using this database source enabled the building up of a comprehensive picture of what the elite male customers sampled were buying. This was aided by the study of other visual and textual material from the Poole archive, of the trade journal *The Tailor and Cutter*, and of social and economic history texts and psychological and sociological texts, in particular Flugel's *The Psychology of Clothes* and Thorstein Veblen's *The Theory of the Leisure Class* (Flugel 1930; Veblen 1994 [1899]). Surviving garments in the Poole archive and in the dress collections of the Victoria and Albert Museum and the Museum of London were also studied in order to help flesh out in visual and tactile form the nature of the objects described in the sales ledgers. This research highlighted the fact that collecting policies have been influenced by the all-pervasive ideas of Flugel, but was nevertheless important in helping to trace the socio-cultural meanings of clothing that survives almost exclusively in the form of historical textual descriptions.

Poole and the Changing Elite Wardrobe

When Henry Poole died, his obituary in *The Tailor and Cutter* of 11 May 1876 read "Mr. Poole was the head of the most noted tailoring firm in the world, both on account of its extent and the aristocratic element in its connection. He was tailor by appointment to all the crowned heads in the world of any note." The firm was founded by James Poole (1781–1846), who by 1806–12 had set up a draper's shop in Everett Street, London.[3] The business subsequently prospered as a military tailor's, and by 1822 James Poole had opened premises at 171 Regent Street (*The Tailor And Cutter*, 15 July 1897: 357). He sub-let this showroom in 1828, and began trading from Nos. 4 and 5 Old Burlington Street, of which he owned the freehold.[4] Although he was successful enough to trade from a fashionable district, he did not attain the heights, both commercial and social, his son Henry (1814–1876) was to reach after inheriting the business in 1846. Henry renamed the company after acquiring ownership, and established the firm in Savile Row itself (Figure 1); the company retains the title of Henry Poole and Co. to this day.

The current premises of Henry Poole and Co. at No. 15 Savile Row were until 1883 home to the Savile Club.[5] Masculine institutions were a distinct feature of the area in the late nineteenth century, as Roy Porter comments: "Clubs helped keep London a masculine city, and St. James's, with its bachelor chambers around King and Jermyn Streets, was its inner sanctum" (Porter 1994: 282). This gendering of the district meant

Figure 1
Photograph of the exterior of Henry Poole and Co.'s premises in Savile Row, dated between 1869–1903, courtesy of Henry Poole and Co.

gentlemen could step out of their lodgings and visit their club, hat-maker, gun-maker, boot-maker or tailor in the course of a leisurely promenade.[6]

This picture is in direct contrast to the increasingly feminized historical analysis of fashionable consumption and retailing that has underpinned most discussions of modernizing developments in the late-nineteenth-century clothing industry and its associated urban retail environments. In contrast to ready-to-wear and made-to-measure manufacturing and the newly sophisticated world of department store retailing, high-class bespoke tailoring remained an almost exclusively masculine domain throughout the nineteenth century (Schmiechen 1984; Schwartz 1992). Poole's customers would have enjoyed guaranteed entry to an all-male environment (apart from the extremely occasional glimpse of the rare female customer), and could be sure that their garments would be scarcely touched by the female hand or influenced by the feminine gaze until they first stepped out in public in their newly crafted clothing. Allegations that women had contributed to the sewing of garments were hotly denied by all the best West-End firms, as women were not allowed to train as tailors and were therefore regarded as unskilled labor (*The Tailor and Cutter*, 22 and 29 July 1897; Schmiechen 1984). The application of the finer aesthetic judgement of women to the clothing choices of men has been assumed in most literature on nineteenth-century consumption to date. However, a range of articles in the *Tailor and Cutter* of the period that warn cutters to avoid the attendance of wives at fittings at all costs suggests that on most occasions the choice of the finer details of male fashion was exclusively a male pursuit (*The Tailor and Cutter*, 1868–1900). This therefore positions Poole's as both a class-based space and a gendered space within which the social and sartorial identities of their customers were negotiated via the individualized and collaborative design process, peculiar to bespoke tailoring. It was this design and manufacturing process that prevailed within Henry Poole and Co. in the late nineteenth century.

In bespoke tailoring a garment is ordered before it is made, so the beginning of the sales process is also the beginning of the design process. This involves deciding on the cut, style features, cloth and trimmings to be used. For nearly all orders between 1861 and 1900 Poole's provided the cloth and the trimmings. Company literature and customer letters reveal that orders were placed either in person at the shop, through visits to customers' homes, by letter, or through traveling representatives who received customers at foreign hotels.

The initial design process (garments would evolve through a series of fittings, but the main characteristics would be decided on at the ordering stage) involved the customer and either a cutter, a salesman or a traveling representative. The dynamics involved in this collaborative design process were largely determined by how aware and forthright the customer was as to his wishes, with the professionals adapting according to the individual concerned. A broad range of scenarios was possible, as is revealed by an article in *The Tailor and Cutter* of 29 March 1888, which reported that the "Duke of Portland has, I hear, just designed a uniform for himself as Master of the Horse" and the somewhat contradictory fact that Poole's were renowned as designers of both civil uniforms and court dress.[7]

The bespoke process of designing and making was therefore not at all straightforward, and was made even more complex and ambiguous by the shifting tensions between late-nineteenth-century class identities, masculinities and fashion. Henry Poole and Co. not only had to negotiate these wider tensions successfully; they had also to appeal to a range of individual tastes, from the deeply conservative to those of the most fashionable men in London society.

Surveying a list of Poole's notable customers of the later nineteenth century confirms the firm's position at the head of the West End bespoke trade and the international nature of their almost exclusively male clientele.[8] Poole and Co. were patronized by a range of distinguished individuals, from HRH the Prince of Wales to HIM The Emperor of Russia. However, by contrast with the popular image of nineteenth-century Savile Row firms as catering only to titled customers, the firm's clientele also included a substantial number of commoners of a variety of occupations and sources of wealth. British customers came from metropolitan as well as provincial locales, and international customers came from a diverse range of mainly Western or colonized countries. The one characteristic they all shared was a desire to dress at "the most noted tailoring firm in the world" and sufficient funds to pay the high prices Poole's charged for their top-quality garments (*The Tailor and Cutter*,

11 May 1876). This leads to the correct but rather crude conclusion that the bulk of Poole's customers in 1861 and 1900 may be identified as "elite" in terms of income and social status. In the following section this category will be broken down into more meaningful terms; but first it is useful to discuss what type of clothing these "elite" men bought from Poole's in 1861 and 1900.

A focus on case studies of two individuals not only reveals the contents of their wardrobes, but also assists in consideration of the types of social elite they represent. Earl Dunmore, the 1861 customer, typifies old wealth and the British aristocratic tradition; while the 1900 customer, Mr Drayton J. Coleman of 67 Wall Street, New York, represents the increased prominence of untitled new money and American financiers in the reformulated turn-of-the-century international elite. Whilst this choice of different types of customer does not allow for a direct comparison of like with like, it does directly reflect changes within Poole's clientele. The small group of customers who were purchasing most shifted from titled British patricians in the main in 1861 to principally the American wealthy in 1900. A further reason for the choice of Earl Dunmore and Mr Drayton J. Coleman is the number and range of their transactions. They probably bought the bulk of their extensive wardrobes from Poole's, and thus represent in concentrated form the "model" customer.

Earl Dunmore's Purchases

Charles Adolphus Murray was born in 1841, and by 1845 he had succeeded his father to become the seventh Earl of Dunmore. His family's listing in *Burke's Peerage and Baronetage* of 1858 reveals that he belonged to a long-established British aristocratic family, that many of his ancestors were military officers, and that his family had close royal links (1858: 339–40). Further research shows that by 1861 the Earl had left Eton College and was an officer in the British regiment of the Scots Fusiliers.[9] In addition, his duties as a landowner would have included responsibility for the family seats of Dunmore Park in the county of Stirling and the Island of Harris, both in Scotland. The Earl's ledger entries contain no details of delivery addresses; however, his titled position and fashionable wardrobe may be taken as almost certain indicators that he spent part of the year in London, as dictated by the etiquette of the London season.

Further clues as to the Earl's social identity may most profitably be gained through a discussion of his 1861 wardrobe. This was an extensive and extremely fashionable affair, and is therefore not typical of the majority of Poole's customers. However, the large number of garments ordered by the Earl facilitates the discussion of the scope of the male elite wardrobe in its broadest sense. Also, the cutting-edge stylishness of the clothing consumed is useful, in that many of the clothing practices featured prefigure later developments in the design of menswear. The range and fashionable nature of the wardrobe also mean that the Earl's clothing choices represent a surprisingly ideal context within which to question

Flugellian, renunciatory interpretations of the late-nineteenth-century male wardrobe. The young Earl's wardrobe features, for example, the classically renunciatory, formal garments of black frock coat and black evening dress tail-coat. However, taken within the context of his proposed lifestyle and wardrobe as a whole, these objects become intrinsically linked with certain social practices, and the notion that they may be taken as universal signifiers of a total lack of male interest in dress becomes simplistic and inaccurate in the extreme.

The Earl of Dunmore's 1861 list of transactions creates a picture of what a young gentleman required in order to fit in with the sartorial etiquette of the London season. He had one hundred and seventeen transactions, from which, for the purposes of this article, fourteen servants' livery transactions and forty-eight clothing maintenance transactions have been deducted, leaving fifty-five new-garment transactions.[10] In order to provide a more meaningful discussion of the clothing purchased, these will first be placed within the context of the social rituals and practices to which they relate.

A young aristocrat taking part in the season in 1861 would have spent the summer months in London and much of the rest of the year at his country seat. Earl Dunmore's personal negotiation of the social season would have been informed by his military commitments. Within this broad pattern, his transactions show a clear relationship with the aristocratic model of what was acceptable for wear at certain times of day, in certain locations and social settings, and to participate in certain types of physical activity. Much has been written about the rituals of the season, particularly in social history texts; however, the role of male fashionable consumption within this has been more or less ignored to date. This has been reinforced by a general acceptance of Flugellian notions that nineteenth-century menswear was almost exclusively dominated by sober, middle-class, ascetic and renunciatory ideals. Closer examination of the 1861 purchases of the Earl of Dunmore reveals contradictions that echo Henry James's description of the London Season in an 1888 edition of the *Century Magazine*. He pronounced "It is a fine, decorous, expensive, Protestant carnival" (James 1888).

The facts that elite menswear was both fashionable in style and etiquette-related are evident on examining the list of Dunmore's 1861 purchases. It becomes clear that although "rules" of sartorial etiquette were extremely important, they were in a constant state of flux as to the specific style, cut, materials and accessories that might "correctly" be worn, although it is broadly true that in 1861 a lounge suit would be acceptable for informal morning wear, a morning coat or frock coat for more formal daywear and a dress tail-coat for evening wear (Breward 1999: 61). The precise nature of these garments and what they might "correctly" be worn with varied according to the specific occasions, which might include anything from social calls and business meetings, to nights at the opera, court appearances, and visits to Ascot, Cowes, Henley, or Goodwood, and to a wide range of participation sports. Sartorial choices were also influenced by whether the clothing was to be worn in winter or summer, country or town, or at home or abroad (Sproule 1978). In simple terms these complex parameters broadly translated into varying degrees of social and sartorial formality. For example, the young Earl Dunmore's formal outfits purchased in 1861 included "A black single melton lounging [morning] coat with silk sleeve linings, a matching vest and a pair of dark gray stripe doeskin trousers" and for evenings "A superfine black dress coat with silk sleeve linings and fancy breast facings, a black cachmere dress vest and a pair of black half doeskin trousers." In addition, two frock coats are mentioned in the Earl's list of maintenance transactions. In winter these garments might have been combined with the fashionable options of "A grey angola cape with wings" or "A light Elysean frock great coat, double-breasted, lined with silk, with a quilted body and back and a silk velvet collar."

Notably, even frock and dress tail-coats, which were relatively more "static" in design than other male clothing of the time, changed between the 1861 and 1900 samples in terms of the materials used and when it was "correct" to wear them. This illustrates the interplay between fashion and supposedly "fixed" systems of sartorial etiquette, which owing to the shifting character of elite society were also a source of change and constant renegotiation. That relationship is further highlighted by an examination of three other types of clothing that are particularly evident in the listing of the Earl's wardrobe: uniforms; sportswear; and outfits to be worn in the private world of the home.

Earl Dunmore's purchases in 1861 included "A superfine blue uniform frock coat with silk skirt linings, trimmed with braid," and "A milled superfine scarlet uniform tunic lined with flannel (own embroidery)." Uniforms were a common feature of aristocratic wardrobes of this period, even if the owner was not a military man, as many patricians held positions that called for or permitted the wearing of civil uniforms. As is discussed by Scott Myerly in his 1996 text *British Military Spectacle*, the elaborate, decorative qualities of uniforms had strong links with elite male fashionable display, and the contemporary male role models of heroic significance were often the British military and colonizing adventurers who shopped at Poole's. Those "heroes" celebrated in popular literature and theater of the period (see Figure 2) were almost always of the "officer class," and thus the glamor and romance of the British adventurer is both elevated from and also integrally connected with notions of class. Thus one may suggest that the wider identification of some Western men with the visual and therefore sartorial language of the English "hero" is a factor that may have aided the persistence of English elite models through the declining years of the nineteenth century. This type of identification goes beyond the more often discussed aspirational content of elite masculine identities towards an arguably much more powerful identification inspired by the type of self-realization afforded by fantasy (Dawson 1991).

PRICE ONE PENNY.] A CRICKET BAT GIVEN EVERY WEEK.

CHUMS

No. 29.—Vol. I.] MARCH 29, 1893. [All rights reserved.

CONTENTS.

THE IRON PIRATE. (*A New Serial Story.*) By Max Pemberton. See pages 454–455.

	PAGE		PAGE
The Wooing of Gudjowra Pulwul ...	450	A Race for Life ...	458
On a Training Ship ...	452	Cycling at Easter ...	459
Our Olla Podrida ...	456	Boxing ...	460
Plain Facts in Natural History (*Full Page Illustration*) ...	457	Two. (*A Serial Story.*) By Barry Pain ...	462
		Jokes, Pictures, etc. etc.	

"'Ah, thank heaven! I have you at last!' cried the Major, running forward." (*See page 451.*)

Figure 2
Illustrated cover of the popular British boys journal *Chums*, March 29, 1893, No.29. Vol. I., by courtesy of The Trustees of the National Library of Scotland. Late nineteenth-century journals of that type often featured military and imperial themes.

Several other items bought by Earl Dunmore suggest links between male fashionable display, class and masculine ideals of the period. Earl Dunmore was evidently a keen sportsman, and his purchases included riding, shooting, yachting and boating attire. In 1861, these sports were almost exclusively upper-class pursuits based around a milieu of wealth and, more specifically, landownership. They were also incorporated into the curriculum of public schools as appropriate training for a life of social and political leadership (Mangan and Walvin 1987). The Earl's utilitarian sporting outfits therefore included "An Eton blue flannel shirt, an Eton blue silk neck tie and a pair of white flannel trousers with a blue stripe."[11] He also ordered "A fancy angola short shooting coat with silk sleeve linings, a matching vest and trousers," "A superfine blue pilot beaver double-breasted yachting jacket, with silk sleeve linings and matching vest and trousers" and "A bright blue diagonal angola double-breasted boating jacket, with a matching vest, trousers and hat." These outfits are illustrative of the Earl's engagement with newly fashionable styles of the period, as well as showing an integral connection with resolutely masculine ideals and activities.

Connotations of a leisured, high-status lifestyle were repeated in Earl Dunmore's purchasing of the following ensemble: "A striped Albanian silk shawl dressing jacket, lined with silk, with a pair of matching silk-lined trousers and a matching silk girdle." This outfit relates strongly to the smoking jackets that have been well documented in dress history texts as evening wear to relax in at home. A focus on the issue of comfort has masked the potential of these garments to throw into question Flugellian interpretations of nineteenth-century menswear and masculinity. In their visual and textural extravagance and intrinsic links with the private world of the home they shatter received notions about nineteenth-century men and fashionable consumption. Other examples of similarly exuberantly colored and sensuously fashioned outfits exist in the Poole's ledgers, including, significantly, outfits purchased by the then Prince of Wales, which suggests that these garments were not just for the effeminate and overly-theatrical male members of the upper class. This evidence adds to the recent findings of Breward and John Tosh, who have questioned the existence of rigidly defined "separate spheres" for late-nineteenth-century men and women, whereby under a system of patriarchy men are intrinsically connected to the public sphere, leaving women as primarily concerned with the domestic sphere (Breward 1999; Tosh 1999).

It is clear from the evidence above that, in contradiction to Flugel's sweeping assertions, it was possible for a nineteenth-century gentleman to be both "correctly" and also "elegantly" and "elaborately" attired (Flugel 1930). However, it must be acknowledged that Earl Dunmore's wardrobe was particularly modish and also that elite male dress codes allowed for wider parameters within which men could experiment, without fear of moral and social censure, than did those of their middle-class counterparts. What is interesting to note is that this greater experimentation was located in specifically defined areas, and that these tended to be spheres defined by their connotations of "manliness."

Mr Drayton J. Coleman's Purchases

Mr Drayton J. Coleman was an untitled American whose main address appears in the Poole ledgers as 67 Wall Street, New York. This address, and the wealth and social status that is evident from his extensive list of transactions, including court dress, indicates with a fair degree of certainty that Mr Coleman was involved in finance. The ledgers also reveal three separate delivery addresses in 1900 of Fair Oak, Rogate, Sussex, 68 Eaton Place, Belgravia, London and the Carteris Hotel, London. Those items not listed against any of the above addresses were probably dispatched to Mr Coleman in New York. This paints Mr Coleman as a frequent visitor to London who either owned, rented or visited a country house close to London and also a town house in London's most exclusive residential district. The pattern of his delivery dates and addresses suggests an engagement with the traditional calendar of the London season and also that Mr. Coleman perhaps took part in the increasingly fashionable practice amongst the reformulated elite of departing for country weekends. Mr Coleman had forty-eight transactions in 1900, from which, for the purposes of this article, seven maintenance transactions and three purchases of packing cases have been deducted, leaving thirty-eight new-garment-based transactions.

Mr Coleman's wardrobe, of some forty years later, is more conservative than Earl Dunmore's, though it is sufficiently in tune with turn-of-the-century trends in male fashion to make it an excellent example for discussion. It also allows for examination of the accuracy of the statement made by Mr. D. Belinfante, a manager of Henry Poole and Co., in an interview with *The New York Herald* of 24 September 1897. He states "I can tell you that an American customer when he orders of an English tailor, expects to get English clothes, English material and English made." Mr Coleman's purchases show that Mr. Belinfante's heartfelt words disguise a more complex picture of change within elite late-nineteenth-century men's fashion. The financier's decision to patronize an English tailor may be taken as simply a personal predilection for the English look. However the list of famous, wealthy Americans who patronized Poole's, let alone the likely overall total who used other West End tailors, suggests that the type of clothing produced for Mr Coleman was representative of wider social practices amongst the American wealthy elite. Through this and other foreign patronage English bespoke tailoring was becoming increasingly international, not just in terms of who wore it but also as influenced by the collaborative nature of the bespoke design process. American influence may be traced in the Poole's sales ledgers through the appearance of lighter weights of cloth, cotton garments for riding and a greater tendency towards unlined lounge jackets. These characteristics may be linked to the practical realities of climactic differences; however, they also represent the subtle extension of the modernization and casualization of the Western male wardrobe. That a typical English look existed throughout the period studied is undeniable; yet the finer details of that look as worn by each individual customer were not by 1900 wholly of English origin.

Mr Coleman's 1900 transactions reveal both close links with the earlier aristocratic sartorial and lifestyle model and also a substantive picture of change between 1861 and 1900. Those garments that appear in tune with the earlier model are "A black diagonal dress coat lined with satin with satin sleeve linings and silk breast facings, with a matching double-breasted vest with three braids and two pairs of matching trousers with braid-trim at the sides" and "A steel half-milled melton hunting coat, lined with flannel." These styles of garments were those that remained most static in design between the 1861 and 1900 samples.

The principal shift that occurred in Mr. Coleman's wardrobe compared to that of Earl Dunmore, also reflected the broad patterns of change between the main samples. This was the re-positioning of the lounge suit from its predominant role as utilitarian sportswear to become everyday informal wear. Mr Coleman's 1900 purchases included three outfits that reflect this change. The garments included "A gray milled cheviot short suit with silk sleeve linings." This would have been suitable for informal town wear. For country and sporting wear Mr Coleman ordered "A fancy mixed milled tweed short lounging jacket with silk sleeve linings, a matching vest, a pair of matching trousers and a pair of matching knickerbockers." A similar type of suit worn by Ferdinand James Baron de Rothschild (1839–1898) features in Figure 3. Knickerbockers were only bought by young fashionables like Earl Dunmore in 1861. However, Poole's sold significantly more of these in 1900. This may in part be due to the increased popularity of shooting between these years, which was linked to changing attitudes towards country life, which increasingly involved short, frequent visits, typified by the weekend shooting party (Cannadine 1996: 354). Further moves towards informality were signaled by Mr Coleman's purchase of "A black diagonal angola dining jacket lined with satin, with satin sleeve linings and silk breast facings."

The lounge suit had by 1900 been adopted by society from the lower levels of the middle class downwards as everyday wear. The contents of the Henry Poole and Co. sales ledgers suggest that its adoption at elite level by 1900 was widespread, but also more complex, in that codes of social formality still existed, but in a more relaxed form. This meant that, under the new reformulated dress codes, a short jacket was now acceptable on an increasing number of occasions. For example, the dinner jacket, which was initially only worn in male company, was worn at informal mixed dinners by 1900. However, a frock coat, morning (lounging) coat and dress coat were still essential purchases. The increasing adoption of the lounge suit (in a variety of forms) was a response to a more democratic, modern style of life. Henry Poole's customers' direct engagement with modernity came through the increased proportion of the wealthy who worked for a living, which led to a re-negotiation of the concept of leisure and also an increased cosmopolitanism that was informed by changes in wealth accumulation and new forms of travel (Cannadine 1996: 391–444).

It is interesting to note that this principal shift occurred either within the sphere of sportswear or under its influence. The importance of sport as a factor in men's fashion change has long been acknowledged, though the reasons for this have not been explored in any depth. Sport was

Figure 3
Photograph of Ferdinand James, Baron de Rothschild (1839–1898) by Lord Battersea, undated, courtesy of the National Portrait Gallery, London. The sitter was a customer of Henry Poole and Co. in the late nineteenth century, though it is not possible to say for certain which firm made the suit worn in the portrait.

one of the areas most strongly associated with the ideals of Victorian masculinity or "manliness." It therefore provided a safe guise within which men could experiment with new forms of clothing without fear of ridicule or the slightest taint of effeminacy (Kestner 1994: 5; Paoletti 1985: 124). Thus an outfit like Mr. Coleman's tweed suit expressed the complex contradictions in class and gender values that aspiring members of the turn-of-the-century elite had to negotiate, although the suit is undoubtedly expressive of the kind of ascetic "muscular manliness" that was a popular turn-of-the-century masculine ideal. Owing to its origins as shooting wear, it also has close links with a leisured and landed lifestyle, which evokes similarly strong connotations of luxury and glamor.

Wealth, Class, Glamor and Change

The period from 1861 to 1900 was one of significant change in class and gender relations. It also saw the rise of a new and reformulated international elite, made up of a far broader set of social groupings than in the mid-century. In the 1861 Poole's customer sample, the international aristocracy represented 31 per cent of the firm's clientele; of this total, 17 per cent had British titles. Cannadine describes the character of the nineteenth-century British aristocracy as the international wealth, social and power elite as follows: "they belonged to what was, before the 1880s, an unrivaled elite, not merely in domestic terms but in comparative terms as well" (Cannadine 1996). Until the 1880s, this wealth was primarily derived from land, and the social and political power that co-existed with it was created and maintained largely through a lifestyle whose leisure was carefully constructed around the social season. The social season has been investigated by the historian Leonora Davidoff in her influential work *The Best Circles*, mainly with regard to its effects on the consuming habits of middle-class women. However, her definition of Society and the season remain helpful to this investigation of elite male fashionable consumption; she states:

> Sociologically, Society can be seen as a system of quasi-kinship relationships which was used to "place" mobile individuals during the period of structural differentiation fostered by industrialization and urbanization. As such it can be understood as a feature of a community based on common claims to status honor which were in turn based on a certain lifestyle. In this historical case such claims were defined as attributes of English ladies and gentlemen. Like all status groups, the traditional aristocratic elite were obsessively concerned with the question of access to their ranks (Davidoff 1986: 15).

The existence of the ritualistic set of social practices and events that constituted the "season," along with self-imposed restrictions on choice of marriage partners in order to protect the system of primogeniture, helped to maintain the status of the British aristocracy until the middle of the nineteenth century as the most closed elite in the world (Davidoff 1986). The overriding power of this mid-century exclusivity may be one of the reasons why the social and sartorial models involved in the London "season" remained influential on male fashionable life and clothing styles through the closing decades of the nineteenth century.[12]

The latter half of the nineteenth century saw a relative decline in British land-based titled incomes. In his 1981 text *Men Of Property*, Rubenstein discusses the foremost challenges to traditional forms of wealth formation: "If the nineteenth-century saw the absolute predominance of landed wealth until surprisingly late in the day, it also witnessed the overtaking of landowners by businessmen even at the very peak of the wealth scale." He identifies this process as occurring "from the mid-nineteenth-century" and acknowledges that although

> there were indeed a substantial number of wealthy fortunes in certain manufacturing and industrial trades like cotton manufacturing and engineering, the wealthy in Britain have disproportionately earned their fortunes in commerce and finance—that is, as merchants, bankers, shipowners, merchant bankers and stock and insurance agents and brokers, rather than in manufacturing or industry (1981: 61).

This British-based shift towards commerce and finance as the leading source of large incomes was accompanied by similar and more significant shifts in an international context. Together these contributed to substantial changes in the composition of the international elite by the turn of the century. A significant factor in this scenario was the emergence of a newly powerful American elite, which inspired Thorstein Veblen to write *The Theory of the Leisure Class* and on which Cannadine comments as follows:

> When they had been the richest elite in the western world, the grandees (and gentry) of Britain had bought from impoverished continental aristocrats. But now they in turn had become relatively impoverished, and a new and even richer elite had come into being across the Atlantic, appropriately dubbed by Berenson the "squillionaires" (Cannadine 1996: 112).

These changes were directly reflected in the shifting composition of Poole's clientele, as is shown by a comparison of the 1861 and 1900 customer samples. The principal changes between the two were a decline in foreign titled clientele, a rise in European diplomatic clientele, and the continued presence of the British aristocracy, though they were purchasing significantly less. Also evident was the influx of American custom, which by 1900 dominated the small group who engaged in the greatest numbers of transactions (between 48 and 137 in a year). In 1861 all the customers in this group were British, and four of them were titled individuals. Whereas in 1900 none of the group was titled, only one was British, and two gave addresses in the United States. Some of these changes may be simply due to factors specific to Henry Poole and Co. However, it is notable that they mirror the changes in wealth distribution in the last two decades of the nineteenth century outlined above.

Economic changes clearly played an important part in precipitating the rise of a new and reformulated international elite. However, under the established systems of Society, social status and social connections were the prime route of entry, and this should have led to the outright exclusion of newly wealthy commoners. What in fact took place in the late nineteenth century was a struggle to renegotiate what it meant to be part of the upper class or the "elite." The principal location of this struggle was around the lifestyle and social practices of the season and the question of marriage. These developments raise two important questions: firstly, why those of unprecedented new wealth and power appeared to wish to "play by the old rules"; and secondly, whether it is appropriate to consider their engagement with English "Society" in such simplistic emulative terms.

The sales ledgers and commercial practices of Henry Poole and Co. are useful in revealing that this renegotiation of class identities was played out to a significant extent within the sphere of male fashionable identities, and that a complex intermingling of the priorities and preoccupations of individuals from a diverse range of incomes, occupations, religions and social backgrounds was involved. That this evolved as something more complex than a simple struggle between the titled patrician landowner in his formalized, codified wardrobe and the newly wealthy plutocrat in a range of democratically inspired, modern lounge suits has been made clear in the last section.

Henry Poole and Co. were successful in attracting a diverse range of elite customer types between 1861 and 1900. In that period the firm's clientele included several members of the plutocratic Jewish Rothschild family, as well as many British aristocrats of traditional patrician lifestyles, imperialist professionals from Viceroys of India to military officers, "golden age" New Yorkers like William C. Whitney and John Pierpoint Morgan, industrialists from the North of England like Joseph Whitworth and also doctors and clerics from the wealthy professional classes. This list suggests Henry Poole and Co. catered to all strata of that shifting, crumbling and reconstituting entity of the nineteenth-century international social elite. It further suggests that the firm's ability to help customers negotiate a complex series of social boundaries and codes, which were constantly undergoing subtle but sometimes devastatingly important changes, was crucial to their unrivaled success during the period.

The key role that high-class tailors played in advising customers on social coding is highlighted by the following quote from *The Gentleman's Magazine of Fashions, Fancy Costume and the Regimentals of the Army* in its first edition of 1 May 1828:

> As a passport to good society, dress is equally necessary with address; for although, in some respect, manners make the man, still do we not also appreciate his taste, and fix his standard in genteel life by his good habits? Consequently, his tailor is quite as necessary and influential an ally as even the schoolmaster "armed with his primer" (Walker 1988: 35).

The specificity of the material available in the Poole archive reveals that although the model of the nineteenth-century English aristocratic gentleman's wardrobe was extremely important, the actual consumption practices of elite men in the late nineteenth century were much more diverse and subject to change than has hitherto been recorded. T. H. Escott, writing in 1885, highlights the influence of changes in the newly wealthy upper-middle class on the increasingly variegated composition and lifestyle of the upper orders through the following description of the lifestyle of "the great merchant or banker of today . . . an English gentleman of a finished type."

> If he is not a peer, the chances are that he is a member of the House of Commons. He is a man of wide culture, an authority upon paintings, or china, or black-letter books, upon some branch of natural science, upon the politics of Europe . . . He goes into the City as punctually as his junior clerks; and when he returns from the City he drops for a few minutes into the most exclusive of West End clubs. His grandfather would have lived with his family above the counting house and regarded a trip to Hyde park as a summer day's journey. As for the descendant, his town house is in Belgravia or Mayfair. He occupies it for little more than six months out of the twelve and during the rest of the year lives in his palace in the country . . . There is in fact, but one standard of "social position" in England, and it is that which is formed by a blending of the plutocratic and aristocratic elements (Breward 1999: 77–8).

It is important to remember that this "blending" also occurred through an increasing professionalization of the English aristocracy, which brought that section of society into regular contact, not only with upper-middle-class manners and morals, but also with the modern, urban workplace. A different type of uneasy "blending" between the traditional patrician model lifestyle and new symbols of modernity, such as frequent international travel, new forms of transport and the accelerated consumption of new forms of luxury goods became the indulgences of sons from those titled families who retained the necessary level of wealth. J. M. Lee highlights the early twentieth-century manifestation of these social and moral developments, which were well underway by 1900:

> A greater threat to the established pattern of behavior . . . was the alteration in the standard of manners which opportunities for travel had brought to the upper classes. The next generation of young aristocrats . . . were accustomed to new habits of leisure . . . The age of the motor car and the private yacht, the weekend in Paris and the polo season in Monte Carlo, did not breed the solid worth which the . . . previous generation had expected (Lee 1963: 42).

The frequent appearance of international customers in Poole's sales ledgers of 1900 suggests that travel had even wider repercussions for the shifting elite male fashionable identities of the late nineteenth century. The gentlemanly model, which was central to the ethos of Britain's imperial, "civilizing" endeavors and whose codes of behavior had become inscribed on the power structures of many countries, was also inscribed on the bodies of many elite men from a diverse range of countries. It must be acknowledged, however, that this process happened within the context of other competing class and masculine models. The singular nature of the bespoke design process meant that despite the dominance of what were initially English clothing styles, an active process of three-way cultural exchange was at work, between Poole's employees, their British customers and foreign gentlemen. Although this process crystallized sartorially within Poole's premises, it was also reflective of the international appeal of the English social season, which meant that throughout the late nineteenth century London was patronized as an imperial center of power, wealth, style and influence. Tailors who traded in the ultra-fashionable shopping area around Savile Row were doubtless influenced by the scenario witnessed by a contemporary commentator in *London Of To-day* (1888): "London has become the pleasure lounge for the idlers of the globe. Americans, Frenchmen, Germans, Indians, Colonials and persons of leisure and wealth from all parts of the world flock to the capital city during the season" (Porter 1994: 280–1). This picture of the exchange across a range of national, masculine and class identities, based around English aristocratic social and sartorial models, is underlined by the fact that Henry Poole and Co. had by the early twentieth century branches in Paris, Vienna and Berlin.

Conclusion

This article has shown through analysis of the design, making and consumption of tailored garments from Henry Poole and Co. 1861–1900 that elite male fashionable consumption of the late nineteenth century was concerned not only with the more prosaic aspects of social status, such as income, family origins and professional standing, but also with the more intangible, but equally powerful factors of luxury, glamor and romanticism. It is also crucial to acknowledge that these aspects identified here as a key part of the lingering appeal of the English aristocratic "model" lifestyle and its associated sartorial practices were themselves in flux. They were not only connected to the declining power, wealth and social exclusivity of the traditional elite, but also intermingled with the popular and contradictory "manly" values of sobriety and asceticism. The clothing consumption patterns revealed indicate that recent critiques of Veblen's ideas on social emulation are inadequate to trace and understand the contradictory tensions involved in late-nineteenth-century masculine consumption, whereby moves towards informality and social democratization existed alongside the lingering power and status appeal of a declining social group (Veblen 1994 [1899]). The study has also underlined the value of object-centered archival methodology, which here has enabled contestation of what have been all-pervasive theories, namely those of the existence of separate gendered spheres and of the "Great Masculine Renunciation" (Flugel 1930). This article, with its focus on aristocratic, plutocratic and upper-middle-class consumers, has added to recent work on middle-class male fashionable consumption that has begun to form new theoretical approaches to the study of nineteenth-century male dress (Breward 1999; Tosh 1999). Future research is needed to extend this process by examining its implications not only for the study of men's dress in other periods, but for our understanding of the binary relationship between men's and women's dress from the late eighteenth century onwards.

Acknowledgments

Grateful thanks are due to Dr. Christopher Breward for encouragement, advice and support throughout the writing of my MA dissertation and this article. Sincere thanks are also due to my other MA Dissertation Supervisor, Mr. John Styles, in particular for his assistance in setting up the computer database. Finally, I wish offer the greatest of thanks to Mr. Angus Cundey of Henry Poole and Co. and Miss Avril Hart, formerly of the Victoria and Albert Museum, without whom the study would not have happened.

Notes

1. A case-study of "Henry Poole and Co. Savile Row Tailors 1861–1900" was undertaken as the topic for the author's unpublished Royal College of Art/Victoria and Albert Museum MA dissertation in the History of Design. The material in the Poole archive that formed the basis of that study and this article has not yet been formally archived.
2. The two years 1861 and 1900 were chosen as the main focus for study, and entries were recorded for two complete years. As the records are so vast, samples were taken from the sales ledgers by recording 1,000 transactions each for the years 1861 and 1900, for surnames beginning with C and D only.
3. Three items in the Poole archive refer to this—a letter from Mr. Angus Cundey of 13 May 1994 states "I am not exactly certain of the date that James Poole left Shropshire and came to Everett St, Brunswick Square, but we have various lease assignments dated from 1806 and one of 1812 mentions J. Poole." A letter from Coutts Bank says "Our new account register (of 15th February 1819) describes him as 'tailor and draper of 7 Everett St, Russell Square'." According to his birth

certificate, Henry Poole was born on 8 November 1814 at Everett St, St Georges and Bloomsbury.

4. Survey of London, section on Nos. 36–39 Savile Row, draft copy 1963 in the Poole archive.
5. Westminster Public Library D. 340. This gentlemen's club was resident at No. 15 from 1871 to 1883.
6. For clubs, see Irwin 1920. Among hat-makers, Thomas Hawkes was at No. 14 Piccadilly from 1790; among gun-makers, Mr Mortimer, later of Meyer & Mortimer, tailors, traded as a gun-maker in the area in the early nineteenth century; among boot-makers, John Lobb Ltd, bespoke shoe and bootmaker, has been at St James's Street since 1866. For tailors, see Walker 1988.
7. Source: Poole archive and museum labels from the Dressing The Part exhibition held at the Victoria and Albert Museum in 1997.
8. The firm made a small amount of clothing for women, the bulk of which was paid for by men on their accounts, though a few aristocratic exceptions appear in the ledgers.
9. Information from the Librarian at Eton College Archive and Library states that Earl Dunmore attended the College from 1854 to 1857. He subsequently went straight into the army, acting as a Captain in the Scots Fusiliers.
10. The expression "clothing maintenance transactions" is used to denote those that involve the scouring, cleaning, pressing, repairing and altering of garments.
11. This ledger entry implies that it was acceptable practice for former pupils of Eton College to continue to wear the school colors for sporting activities after their school careers had ended.
12. This contradictory proposition of the lingering power of a declining exclusivity is lent weight by Christopher Breward's study *The Hidden Consumer* (1999), which reveals that despite a relative increase in social mobility and social democratization after 1860, concepts of exclusivity and status increased in importance as factors in the consumption of fashion by middle-class men.

References

Anderson, Fiona. 1998. "Henry Poole And Co. Savile Row Tailors, 1861–1900." Unpublished RCA/V & A MA dissertation.

Breward, Christopher. 1999. *The Hidden Consumer: Masculinities, Fashion and City Life, 1860–1914*. Manchester: Manchester University Press.

Burke's Peerage and Baronetage. 1858. London: Harrison and Sons.

Cannadine, David. 1996. *The Decline And Fall Of The English Aristocracy*. London: Papermac.

Davidoff, Leonora. 1986. *The Best Circles: Society, Etiquette and the Season*. London: Century Hutchinson.

Dawson, Graham. 1991. "The Blond Bedouin: Lawrence of Arabia, Imperial Adventure and the Imagining of English–British Masculinity." In J. Tosh and M. Roper (eds), *Manful Assertions: Masculinities in Britain since 1900*. London: Routledge.

Escott, T. H. 1885. *England: Its People, Polity and Pursuits*. London: Chapman and Hall, quoted in Christopher Breward. 1999. *The Hidden Consumer: Masculinities, Fashion and City Life, 1860–1914*. Manchester: Manchester University Press.

Flugel, J. C. 1930. *The Psychology Of Clothes*. London: The Hogarth Press.

Henry Poole and Co., sales ledgers O and Q, 1861, entries for Earl Dunmore.

Henry Poole and Co., sales ledger C–D 8, 1900, entries for Drayton J. Coleman.

Irwin, A. 1920. *Piccadilly In Three Centuries*. London: Macmillan.

Kestner, Joseph A. 1994. *Masculinities In Victorian Painting*. London: Scolar Press.

Lee, J. M. 1963. *Social Leaders and Public Persons: A Study of County Government in Cheshire since 1888*. Oxford: Clarendon Press.

Mangan, J. A. and James Walvin. 1987. *Manliness And Morality: Middle-class Masculinity in Britain and America 1800–1940*. Manchester: Manchester University Press.

Myerly, Scott Hughes. 1996. *British Military Spectacle: From the Napoleonic Wars through the Crimea*. Cambridge, MA: Harvard University Press.

Paoletti, J. 1985. "Ridicule And Role Models As Factors In American Men's Fashion Change 1880-1900." *Costume*, No 29.

Porter, Roy. 1994. *London: A Social History*. London: Penguin.

Rubenstein, W. D. 1981. *Men Of Property: The Very Wealthy in Britain Since the Industrial Revolution*. London: Croom Helm.

Schmiechen, James A. 1984. *Sweated Industries And Sweated Labour*. London: Croom Helm.

Schwartz, Leonard. 1992. *London In The Age Of Industrialisation*. Cambridge: Cambridge University Press

Sproule, Anna. 1978. *The Social Calendar*. Poole, Dorset: Blandford Press.

The Gentleman's Magazine of Fashions, Fancy Costume and the Regimentals of the Army. 1 May 1828. Henry Poole and Co. archive.

The New York Herald. 24 September 1897. Henry Poole and Co. archive.

The Tailor and Cutter. Various editions 1868–1900. Henry Poole and Co. archive and National Art Library, Victoria and Albert Museum, London.

Tosh, John. 1999. *A Man's Place: Masculinity and the Middle Class Home in Victorian England*. New Haven, CT: Yale University Press.

Veblen, Thorstein. 1994 [1899]. *The Theory Of The Leisure Class*. New York: Dover Publications Inc.
Walker, Richard. 1988. *The Savile Row Story: An Illustrated History*. London: Multimedia Books Ltd.

Fashion Theory, Volume 4, Issue 4, pp.427–446
Reprints available directly from the Publishers.
Photocopying permitted by licence only.

Clothes and the Modern Man in 1930s Oxford

Laura Ugolini

Laura Ugolini is a Research Fellow at the University of Wolverhampton, where she is also the Director of the Committee for the History of Retailing and Distribution (CHORD). Her publications include articles on turn-of-the-century male supporters for women's suffrage, and an edited collection (with C.Eustance and J.Ryan), *A Suffrage Reader. Charting Directions in British Suffrage History*, published by Cassell in 2000. Her current research focuses on men's experiences of selling and buying clothes in Britain, *circa* 1880–1939.

In 1934 an advertisement in *The Oxford Times* announced that "rational tailoring" had arrived in town: The Fifty Shilling Tailors had just opened a new shop. This event was presented as more than the prosaic opening of a new branch of a well-known menswear chain store. It was "another step in the spread of a New Idea in men's tailoring." All men who cared both for their clothes and for "their pockets" were invited to call. They would find clothes that were not only in the very latest styles, but also both cheap and of good quality. Cheapness was indeed one of The Fifty Shilling Tailors' main selling points (*The Oxford Times* 25 May 1934; 27 September 1935; 1 November 1935). As with other chain stores, they were careful to emphasize that all men could afford to shop with them, although the low prices were not, it was generally stressed, inconsistent with the provision of good-quality clothing. Montague Burton believed that his own chain of stores had played a vital part in making elegant clothes available to larger sections of the male population than ever before: "We are justly proud in having made a considerable contribution towards making Britain the best dressed country in the world, so far as men are concerned" (Sigsworth 1990: 89).

The claims of chain stores were to some extent confirmed by contemporary observers, who suggested that, by the inter-war period, changes in the production and distribution of clothes had ensured that working-class and lower-middle-class men and women could afford to dress in very similar ways to the better off among the middle class. George Orwell considered that the "manufacture of cheap clothes," as well as "the general softening of manners" had served to tone down "the surface differences between class and class" (Orwell 1965 [1937]: 133). This was the case in both men's and women's clothes. According to one Sheffield engineering worker, thanks to the new chain stores, "whereas previously the rich man had a tailor and the poor man bought his clothes off the peg, it became possible for Jack to be as well dressed as his Master, or very nearly" (Benson 1994: 217).

This supposedly new uniformity in dress was viewed with some ambivalence by most (non-working-class) commentators. The new "democracy" of cheap and easily accessible consumer goods made available by stores such as Woolworth's was one of the themes explored by J. B. Priestley in his influential *English Journey*, first published in 1934. For the first time, "Jack and Jill are nearly as good as their master and mistress." According to Priestley, though, the new consumer goods were simply too cheap: "too much of it is simply a trumpery imitation of something not very good even in the original. There is about it a rather depressing monotony" (Priestley 1997 [1934]: 325–6). In a more positive vein, Lord Elton observed in his autobiography that it was the clothing of "the underpaid, hat-touching wage-earners" of his boyhood that had been drab and uniform. He commended the transformation of the workers of the past, "with their class-uniforms of coarse, ill-fitting Sunday black, into the independent young artisan in week-end plus-fours" (Elton 1938: 253).

* * *

Despite these claims, the notion of a new inter-class homogeneity in inter-war clothing should be treated with a degree of caution, as the experiences of a certain David Henry Campbell can help to show. On the night between 25 and the 26 of February 1932, the 21-year-old Campbell broke into the tailoring shop of Castell & Son, in one of Oxford's premier shopping streets, and stole clothing to the value of £1.10s. The stolen items included a jacket, trousers and a bathing suit. There is little doubt that Campbell's subsequent discovery and arrest were aided by the unemployed bricklayer's decision to wear the stolen clothes while residing at Stratton St Mary Public Institution (*The Oxford Times* 15 April 1933). By wearing garments intended for University undergraduates, rather than those suitable for a young man living on the margins of society, Campbell had made himself conspicuous, and had attracted the unwelcome attention of the law. His example may very well be an extreme one; and yet it seems a healthy reminder that despite the spread in the inter-war years of cheap, mass-produced ready-to-wear clothing of reasonably good quality, dress remained an important indicator of status and identity. Boundaries of "correct" dress had not entirely broken down.

What remains unclear, though, is the exact nature and extent of these boundaries. The emphasis in recent fashion histories has been on the relative "relaxation" of men's clothing after the First World War, with the abandonment of the stiff formality of the frock coat and of starched collars, in favor of the adoption—at least outside "business hours"—of lighter materials and the more relaxed style of lounge suits, pullovers and soft collars (Byrde 1979: 92; Chenoune 1993: 163–4; de Marly 1985: 125–8). Such an approach, though, while indicative of changing notions of "correct" attire, does not shed light on the relationship between masculine identities and the purchase and consumption of clothes outside a narrow elite, and in the context of the mass production and distribution of menswear. Furthermore, while Christopher Breward and Frank Mort have explored the meanings of fashionable, consuming masculinities in the pre-First World War and post-Second World War periods, the inter-war years have received little attention (Breward 1999; Mort 1996).

This article, therefore, aims to shed some light on this period, and to explore the meanings attached to men's clothes in 1930s Oxford. Using the example of Oxford students and car workers, it will consider the role played by clothing in establishing and reinforcing male group identities. It will question whether, and on what terms, by the 1930s such identities could be defined as "commercialized," and will suggest that consumers were not simply manipulated by retailers and other commercial forces. Using material ranging from local newspapers and periodicals to memoirs, from fictional accounts to "ephemeral" advertising material, this article seeks to provide a snapshot of male clothing styles and patterns of consumption, which takes into account the distinctions between representations (in retailers' adverts, newspaper reports, fictional accounts, and so on) and self-representations (through undergraduate publications, autobiographical accounts, and so on), devoting particular attention to the ways in which all discourses—whether originating from retailers, from supposedly disinterested observers, or from the car workers and students themselves—made inventive use of notions of "modern" and "traditional." Indeed, as a meeting-place between the scholars and citizens of an ancient University town, and the workers in a "modern" car industry, 1930s Oxford provides a powerful picture of the interplay between status and consumption, tradition and modernization that challenges easy generalizations about the relationship between clothing and masculine identities.

* * *

It has become almost a cliché to comment that in the period following the First World War, Oxford rapidly became a city of startling contrasts. Alongside its roles as the home of an ancient and venerable University and as a thriving market town, it had also by the 1920s acquired the role of an industrial center, with the establishment in Cowley, on the eastern side of Oxford, of Morris Motors and later of Pressed Steel. By 1939, although 19.2 per cent of adults were still employed in domestic service, mostly in connection with the University, roughly 30 per cent were now being employed by the motor industry. Less than 1 per cent had been so employed before the First World War (Whiting 1983: 8–10).[1]

Unsurprisingly, the creation of a new identity for Oxford as an industrial town was neither uncontroversial nor uncontested. The changes—both real and perceived—brought by the growth of the motor industry were widely understood in terms of the arrival of the "modern" world to the city. The timelessness of the Oxford of the early 1920s, described by the novelist Evelyn Waugh as a city in whose "spacious and quiet streets men walked and spoke as they had done in Newman's day," had by the 1930s in the eyes of many been "submerged . . . and obliterated" (Waugh 1980 [1945]: 23). The modernization of Oxford has most often been characterized, both by contemporary and by more recent commentators, as an attack on the very material fabric of the city, which by the 1930s was being ruined in order to cater for a new brand of consumer. Industrialization and changing patterns of consumption and modernization were understood as advancing hand in hand. In particular, the disappearance of the small independent shopkeeper, replaced by multiple stores, was seen as the direct result of the incursion into the city of industrial workers. In her history of Oxford, Ruth Fasnacht lamented what she saw as the dominant trend of the inter-war period: the demolition or "modernization" of buildings, in order to "make way for something considered more likely to appeal to the majority of the new working-class citizens." In Cornmarket, one of the city center's main shopping streets, individual shops had been crowded out by branches of multiple stores, "with shop fronts (and with stocks) exactly similar to those found in five hundred other towns" (Fasnacht 1954: 213; Morris 1987 [1965]: 33; Sinclair 1931: 42).

The arrival of a modern world of consumption was heralded not only by chain stores, car parks or the "garishness . . . of big London-controlled enterprises," but was also symbolized by the presence on the main shopping thoroughfares of the car workers themselves, carrying on their persons the fruits of their reprehensible purchasing habits. "The pale-faced mechanics in Oxford bags and tweed coats [who] walk down the Cornmarket" were complicit, according to John Betjeman, in the destruction of Oxford (Betjeman 1990 [1938]: 9). And yet, a further exploration of the meanings attached to men's clothing in 1930s Oxford shows a more complex picture than a simple assault upon "tradition" by mechanics dressed in modern mass-produced finery, as local retailers adopted the language of "modernization" in order to capture the custom of University students, rather than that of car workers.

* * *

It seems clear that to some extent at least, despite claims of homogeneity, the cost, value and quality of clothes remained visible and important indicators of social status. As Ernest Baker remarked, having visited Oxford after an absence of twenty-five years, "caste and humbug" continued to be rampant, and the only way to ensure civil behavior on the part of residents was by wearing a 50s plus-four suit (*The Oxford Times* 20 May 1932). J. G. Sinclair expressed himself with even greater asperity, claiming that "Class distinctions in Oxford are as numerous as the legs on a centipede. And as active. A mere shade in the color of your spats sets up a subtle social standard" (Sinclair 1931: 31).

Nevertheless, the role of clothing does not seem for the most part to have been that of exhibiting one's own, or assessing others' social status and wealth. It also does not seem to have been that of decoding others' private character and moral standing. Indeed, the role of clothing in marking out the individual man from the anonymous urban crowd, either on economic or on moral grounds, seems on the whole to have been hardly in evidence (Gunn 1999: 17–18; Sennett 1974: 20–2; Veblen 1994 [1899]: 103–15). Elizabeth Wilson has suggested that in nineteenth-century Britain, fashion served as a form of classification: "Individuals participated in a process of self-docketing and self-announcement, as dress became the vehicle for the display of the unique individual personality" (Wilson 1985: 155). There are indications that by the inter-war period the role of clothing had shifted, and had become the means of marking the individual's entry into a more or less well-defined male group. To return briefly to Campbell's experiences as a thief, it is unlikely that the stolen clothes gave him away because they were very expensive (they were not), but rather because they did not "fit" with his role as an unemployed down-and-out. As George Orwell remarked of his experiences as a tramp, one only needed to wear the "right clothes" to become one of the "fraternity," other factors, such as accent, being of far less importance. While begging at back doors, his educated voice never gave him away: "I was dirty and ragged and that was all they saw" (Orwell 1965 [1937]: 155). In the same way, by wearing clothing inappropriate to the group he belonged to, Campbell ultimately gave himself away. Campbell's vicissitudes were of course not typical of the experiences of most Oxford men. Nevertheless, they do suggest that notions of group, rather than individual, identity might be a useful way of approaching the question of clothing and masculine status.

Historians have most readily identified the importance of clothing as expressing a sense of belonging to a male "group" in the context of studies of youth and of work-based cultures. Examples have ranged from the notorious Napoo gang in pre-First World War Manchester, with its distinctive uniform of navy blue suit, trilby hat and pink neckerchief, borrowed from American gangster films (Fowler 1992: 144), to the emblematic figure of the nineteenth-century dustman, with his fantail hat, light jacket, breeches, and colorful stockings (Maidment 1998). Despite these studies, the dynamics of the connection between membership of a male group and the purchase, consumption and display of clothing need further exploration, particularly in terms of the "commercialization" that this connection is considered to have entailed in the inter-war period (Davies 1992: 97; Fowler 1992). This article focuses on two such male "consumer groups" in Oxford: University undergraduates and car workers. In their case, the development of distinctive clothing styles served to reinforce bonds created by belonging to the same larger body, be it the University (with its associations of tradition and venerability) or the car factory (with its connotations of brashness and modernity), in the context of contemporary debates about the development of inter-war Oxford as a "modern" city.

* * *

Undergraduates and ex-undergraduates recognized the importance of appropriate clothing in marking the assumption of the role of students. Donald Willis was a working-class Oxford youth who successfully competed for a University scholarship. He marked the transition from Cowley to University by opening an account with Walters, a tailoring and outfitting business that specialized in University custom, where he was fitted for his first evening dress and dinner jacket, and acquired a suit of plus-fours (Willis 1987: 71). With characteristic acidity, J. G. Sinclair emphasized that essential for social success in Oxford, alongside things like "a repertoire of pornographic stories . . . and an exhaustless capacity for suppurating self-conceit" was the possession of at least one pair of plus-fours. He considered that there was a good deal of pressure upon undergraduates to adopt a uniform style of clothing, so that even the Ruskin College student soon discarded "his colliery trousers, or, as the case may be, his porter's cap" and dashed out to buy a pair of flannel trousers (Sinclair 1931: 10, 98).

Trousers (either plus-fours or wide-bottomed flannels), pullovers, college scarves, soft collars and shapeless jackets were the essentials of normal male undergraduate day wear: they were of equal, if not greater, importance in defining "the undergraduate" than the cap and gown. The Reverend Morse-Boycott, for example, was struck on a visit to Oxford, not only by the undergraduates' "tattered gowns," but also by their plus fours and "fancy" pullovers, a combination which apparently made them look like "scarecrows" (*The Oxford Times* 23 June 1933). Significantly, the choice and acquisition of clothes seems for the most part to have taken place outside parental control. Angus Wilson, who graduated from Merton College in 1935, stated of his choice of clothes that "for the first time I could buy the clothes I wanted and I knew that I wanted these" (Thwaite 1986 [1976]: 95).

Students' clothing was nevertheless not uniform. With an estimated half of the undergraduates in receipt of some form of financial assistance or scholarship, financial matters alone must have constrained the choice of a considerable number. At the other end of the financial scale "the rich men" seem to have been easily recognizable, not only by their fast and fashionable lifestyle, but also by the fact that "They wear checks. They wear whole suits, well cut . . . They are more often seen in a hat than in cap and gown." Apart from the fact that they must have represented only a tiny minority, it is significant that they were considered to belong more to London, to races and to country houses than to undergraduate Oxford (Betjeman 1990 [1938]: 37). Among the majority of students, individuality seems to have been asserted through the adoption of particular details, rather than a wholesale rejection of the undergraduate outfit. According to John Betjeman, the "aesthetes" of the 1920s, such as Harold Acton, Evelyn Waugh, or Betjeman himself, who had clearly stood out with their "long hair and odd clothes," had by the 1930s disappeared. The aesthete of this decade was "a little scrubby-looking nowadays; his tie alone flames out" (Betjeman 1990 [1938]: 38). Angus Wilson wore the "regulation undergraduate gray flannels, sports coats and umbrellas," but added "canary-colored woolen waistcoats with brass buttons . . . foulard spotted scarves, and a pleasing selection of bottle green maroon and dark crimson velvet ties." The ensemble was not meant as the expression of a unique personality, but "deceptively might have suggested to a stranger that I belonged to a smart Oxford set" (Thwaite 1986 [1976]: 95).

Distinctive clothing was indeed most often associated not with the rejection of the undergraduate identity, but rather with an allegiance to a particular group within it. Items ranged from the ties of particular clubs to sportsmen's outfits. The latter were ridiculed by P.A.S., a contributor to one of the student magazines, who deprecated the way in which sporting undergraduates would in the afternoon change from Harris tweeds, whose "serviceable nature" no one would dispute, to shorts, ". . . sweaters . . . studded boots . . . multicolored scarves—[which] are vulgar and unnecessary" (*The Isis* 10 May 1933).

Political opinion contributed a further clothing code. Oswald Mosley's black-shirted Fascists were the most obvious example; but it seems clear that all shades of political opinion were attributed a distinctive apparel, even if the reality may have been rather less dramatic. In his advice to first-year students, Michael Sheldon suggested that "If you are a Right politician, a sober suit is suggested, with possibly, a stiff white collar. A red tie is essential for success as a Lansbury . . . and . . . rougher tweeds than usual, and your flannels just cannot be clean" (*The Isis* 13 October 1937). By 1933, concern was being expressed at the apparently growing tendency among undergraduates to wear political "uniforms" (*Oxford Mail* 19 May 1933).

The wearing of politically-motivated clothing was perceived as an exclusively University phenomenon, although in fact this represented one of the exceptional occasions when Town and Gown can be seen to have shared a common clothing code. On May Day 1933, for example, a meeting of "Oxford reds" was held in the Oxford Town Hall, with the aim of forming a uniformed body to defend their meetings against Fascist attacks. Among those present were representatives of both City and University organizations: the Oxford Trades and Labor Council, the Oxford City Labor Party and the University Labor Club among others. It was decided that the wearing of some form of uniform had become a necessity. Although the color was never in doubt, there was disagreement as to the nature of the uniform, with some arguing for a red leather jerkin or pullover, while others considered a (red) badge on the arm sufficient. The need for uniforms was expressed in purely practical terms: "In the case of a rough and tumble, you want to know you are not bashing the chap on your side" (*Oxford Mail* 2 May 1933). In the sense of establishing a group identity, the motives for wearing a political uniform do not seem to differ from those lying behind the wearing of the distinctive clothing of the sportsman or the aesthete, or indeed more generally of the undergraduate: identities that were established through acts of consumption.

The dynamics that lead a group, in this case University undergraduates, to adopt a collective identity based on a more or less distinctive clothing style are difficult to disentangle. While in cases such as that of the Napoo gang, the influence of contemporary cinema is easy to detect, in the case of students the relationship with commercial forces is a more complex one. Indeed, films such as *A Yank at Oxford* (1938) seem to have exploited—and possibly reinforced—existing images of undergraduate life and style (Richards 1989 [1984]: 316); it was retailers who had a more direct impact on students' fashionable consumption.

* * *

Despite the strong connection made by commentators between developments in retailing and the arrival of car workers, there is little doubt that outside East Oxford, traders' (including menswear retailers') main strategy continued to be to attract University—and in particular undergraduate—custom. Morris Motors could claim that much of the £ 20,000 paid every week in wages to its workers was spent in Oxford shops (*The Oxford Times* 2 October 1931), but there seems to have been a general agreement that the greatest asset to Oxford trade remained its relationship with the University, and particularly with undergraduates (*The Oxford Times* 4 December 1931).

Oxford menswear retailers may have expressed little interest in attracting the custom of industrial workers, but this does not mean that they deprecated the development of a modern commercial identity for Oxford. By the 1930s, it was common among those writing and commenting on the retailing industry to associate—perhaps unthinkingly—independent shopkeepers with notions of the "traditional" and the "old-fashioned," and chain stores with the "modern" (Levy 1948: 89–90). Independent Oxford traders, though, elaborated a distinctive advertising rhetoric, which blended notions of "modernity" and "tradition," and countered the critics of Oxford's "modernization" by projecting an image of themselves as up-to-date enterprises, but respectful of the ancient fabric of the city.

Cowley's shopping area's claim to be the "Most progressive quarter of Oxford" was therefore contested by city center traders (*Oxford Mail* 5 May 1933). The shops in the High Street, one of Oxford's premier shopping areas, were described as "modern emporiums, yet preserving the antiquity of their facades" (*Oxford Monthly* August 1935). The exclusive department store Elliston & Cavell, which in 1933 had established a separate "Shop for men," also claimed to be ". . . an example of modern enterprise allied to restraint in deference to its surroundings" (*The Oxford Times* 20 October 1933). In terms of merchandise, traders were keen to emphasize the way they were able to reconcile "the well-known Oxford quality" (*The Oxford Times* 20 October 1933) with a responsiveness to "modern" trends. Walters, a tailoring and outfitting firm based in a lane off the High Street, was typical of a wider trend in rejecting an exclusive concentration on the bespoke trade. "In keeping with the spirit of the age" they acquired "a huge stock of styles, patterns and sizes" of ready-to-wear clothes.[2]

Significantly, the new chain stores similarly blended their claims to modernity with an emphasis on their respect for tradition. The Fifty Shilling Tailors were an exception in their relentless claims to modernity, and in their claims to be "new" and "up-to-date." Indeed, those men who resisted its blandishments were dismissed as prejudiced and as "afraid to try a new idea" (*The Oxford Times* 22 November 1935). Austin Reed, on the other hand, was more representative of other chain stores. In 1935 the firm bought and renovated the Plough Inn, a building originally dating from the late seventeenth century, and re-opened it as a shop. While stressing the novelty and up-to-date nature of the merchandise for sale, the firm's respect for the fabric of the building was also emphasized: the architects had been given "a free hand to treat the interior of the premises in a style as much in harmony with the original seventeenth century work as possible."[3]

Retailers may have staked their distinctive place in the "modern" Oxford, but it is clear that—as was mentioned above—this was an Oxford still dominated by the rhythm of University life. By the 1930s in Britain as a whole a shopping calendar whereby changes of season were marked by periodic sales and "events" was well established. While this was also the case in Oxford, here menswear and other retailers at the same time developed a shopping calendar closely connected to the academic year. This was true even of shops unlikely to be patronized by members of the

University. In May 1930, for example, the Co-op announced the arrival of "Eights Week" and issued the call: "Everyone in flannels!" (*The Oxford Times* 23 May 1930). More specifically, menswear retailers also developed an iconography that made it clear that undergraduates were the customers they aimed to attract.

Figure 1 shows one of Walters' advertisements. Here it is not so much the gown, crumpled under an arm, but rather the plus-fours, the pullover and the negligently unbuttoned jacket that make it clear that the image on the left is meant to represent a student before his transformation into an elegant businessman (*The Isis* 6 June 1934). With some minor variations, this image remained emblematic of the 1930s undergraduate, whose style and clothing, to which students were expected to adhere, were instantly recognizable.

Figure 1
Walters advert. *The Isis* 6 June 1934. Reproduced by permission of the British Library, shelfm. 327, (Copyright *The Isis*).

It remains open to question whether styles of undergraduate clothing were informed and influenced by retailers' adverts. Historians—among others—continue to debate the impact of advertising, and of commercial forces in general on consumers' decision-making (Breazeale 1994; Greenfield, O'Connell and Read 1999; Marchand 1985: 238–54; Mort and Thompson 1994). For periods before the advent of consumer surveys (which have themselves been shown to be blunt instruments), it is practically impossible to determine the relative impact on consumer choice and on personal taste of "commercial" forces, such as advertising or cinema, and economic factors, such as the accessibility and price of goods. In his study of pre-Second World War working-class culture in Manchester and Salford, Andrew Davies has suggested that "corner lads" was the most common description of young men, "reflecting the centrality of street activities in youth culture as late as the 1930s." It also suggests a pattern of group identity defined by activities other than the purchase and consumption of goods. In the case of Oxford undergraduates, on the other hand, consumption patterns—and in particular, the purchase and use of certain clothes—were of overwhelming importance in creating and sustaining a separate identity (Davies 1992: 97).

In this sense, undergraduates' identity was a "commercial" one. This does not mean that they were in any simple sense "manipulated" by retailers. Rather, their relationship seems to have been an uneasy one of mutual dependence, a relationship in which power cannot be stated to be overwhelmingly on either side. By the 1930s, Oxford tradesmen had a well-established and notorious reputation for being far too ready to grant long-term credit to undergraduates only recently emancipated from parental control, encouraging them to contract debts from which they could extricate themselves only with the greatest difficulties (Yee 1944: 5). In 1930, the undergraduate journal *The Isis* had been forced, under pressure from the Oxford Chamber of Trade, to apologize for having accused Oxford traders of "cupidity" and "exorbitant prices" (*The Oxford Times* 14 March 1930). In contrast to this image of traders preying upon students, Roger Dataller deprecated "the insidious influence" on townspeople of their dependence on the University for custom. This, he considered, inevitably sapped "the dignity of spirit of a full-grown man." Nevertheless, he himself as a student had been manipulated by a shrewd shopkeeper into paying more than he meant to—in cash—for a lounge coat (Dataller 1933: 95–6; 149).

Boundaries of correct dress were furthermore policed not only by retailers and advertisers. Paul Nystrom has indicated the strength of the forces that compelled men to conform to particular styles of clothing. For those who refused to conform, "There will be quizzical looks, doubtful stares and critical estimates. He will be thought queer. He will be judged as lacking in brain power and, perhaps, as an undesirable person" (Nystrom 1928: 9–10). Although in Nystrom's analysis such opprobrium was seen to originate from a generalized "society," in fact the most powerful indictments of non-conformity could come from the group to which the individual was perceived as belonging. Pressures to conform to certain canons could therefore be found within the undergraduate community itself. The flouting of such canons could lead to punishment, including, in some cases, through physical violence: the "debagging" of aesthetes, or the wrecking of their rooms on the part of athletic "hearties" being an obvious example (Graves and Hodge 1995 [1940]: 124).[4]

Students themselves could present the connection between their identity and particular styles of clothing as a denial of any link with modern commercialism. Their clothing could serve to align them rather with a sense of tradition and of Oxford's past. D. F. Karaka portrayed undergraduates' clothing almost as part of the ancient fabric of the city: ". . . with its Gothic structures and dreamy spires, and that drab gray splashed all over—from buildings to bags—Oxford is still as venerable as the Oxford which Arnold knew" (Karaka 1933: 44). In a more open embracing of "tradition" over the "modern," in May 1931 the editors of *The Isis* and *The Cherwell*, the two main undergraduate magazines, united in announcing their intention of wearing the old-fashioned straw boater while punting on the river as ". . . a symbol of a glorious past." The boater represented more than a connection with tradition. It also represented a way of differentiating the consumption patterns of students from those of the "plebeian masses." "The triumph of the felt hat over the boater" on the river was seen as embodying ". . . the indecorous shrieks of the plebeian masses, whose hired punts plough a laborious way through a Sargasso sea of banana skins . . . [and have] forever banished from the river the white silk shirts and immaculate flannel trousers of the aristocracy" (*The Cherwell* 9 May 1931; *The Isis* 6 May 1931).

* * *

The "plebeian masses" never acquired the same iconic status as undergraduates in their role as consumers of clothing. There is no doubt that the car workers were by the 1930s a visible, and apparently permanent presence on the streets of Oxford, well beyond the confines of the industrial eastern areas. In terms of representations, though, beyond the role as harbingers of "modernity" accorded to them by critics of the city's industrialization, Cowley workers remained far less visible than University undergraduates. In particular, car workers' representation and role as purchasers and consumers of clothes continued to be a marginal one.

To some extent, this "invisibility" reflects the way in which Cowley as a whole remained marginal to representations of Oxford. Alison Light has noted "the adoration which was afforded to all things Oxford between the wars," an adoration reflected for example in the frequency with which the city was used as a setting for the increasingly popular detective fiction of the 1930s (Light 1991: 77–8). Nevertheless, despite the occasional disturbing hints of the presence of "another," less picturesque Oxford—the Coles had their detective, newly arrived from London, remark that the area near the station looked "like a back street of Birmingham"—the "whodunits" of the 1930s focused overwhelmingly on the circumscribed world of the Colleges (Cole and Cole 1938: 87). In a similar way, Cowley is largely absent from most inter-war fiction set in Oxford (Dougill 1998: 168–73).

Cowley workers—and the Oxford working-class as a whole—did not have the same opportunities as those afforded to the University undergraduates for self-representation. Students had avenues such as the undergraduate magazines (although admittedly these did not always necessarily reflect the views of the majority of the student population) to create their own image and identity, as well as to respond to attacks from outside. The satirical response in *The Isis* to Richard Rumbold's lampooning of Oxford's "effeminacy and its young perverts" in the *Sunday Referee* is a case in point (Figure 2. *The Isis*, 26 April 1933). In

Figure 2
"Counterblast." *The Isis* 26 April 1933. Reproduced by permission of the British Library, shelfm. 77 (Copyright *The Isis*).

the case of Cowley workers, representations—as harbingers of modern consumerism and chain stores—dominated over self-representations.

In 1965 college servants told Jan Morris that before the Second World War, the town boys had tried to look like undergraduates (Morris 1987 [1965]: 90). Nevertheless, there are some indications that, at least as far as the car workers were concerned, styles of clothing were developed with little reference to the University. Looking back on her East Oxford youth, Phyl Surman described how car workers would generally wear standard dark suits of trousers, jacket and waistcoat, which could be varied by wearing a pullover instead of a waistcoat, or a silk scarf instead of a collar. Caps would be worn for work, but trilby hats and raglan raincoats on a Sunday (Surman 1992: 68). Clothing also served to mark distinctions and differences in status between the various Cowley workers. Because of the cleaner nature of their work, for example, Morris Motors employees could wear a "respectable" jacket and tie at work, while Pressed Steel men were easily recognizable by their greasy overalls (Whiting 1983: 57). Cleaner work and respectable clothing became enmeshed in creating an image of Morris Motors workers as "superior." Cowley's dynamism and changing nature as a community were further reflected in the adoption of "new fashions" by the local young men. These fashions were not copied from cinema stars, often seen as the main focus of working-class emulation, but rather from Welsh immigrants, newly arrived from depressed mining districts. The new fashion could be seen on Sundays, in the shape of "a smart suit, the most notable feature of which was the double-breasted waistcoat cut straight across the lower front." Significantly, "This style was copied and much favored by the young men but was not approved by their more provincial parents" (Surman 1992: 68).

Despite the relatively high wages that car workers could earn—although irregular, earnings averaged out between 70s. and 80s. per week (Whiting 1983: 40)—in terms of the consumption of fashionable clothing, there is little indication that Oxford retailers outside Cowley made any serious effort to attract their custom. It was left to shops such as the Cowley Road drapery and shoe store Butler's to cater for them, and offer items such as men's khaki shirts as "very suitable for engineers and mechanics," or woolen gloves as "very welcome to cyclists and lorry drivers in wet and cold weather" (*The Oxford Times* 25 September 1931).

Images of working men, or rather of men in working clothes, were extremely rare in adverts in general. Unsurprisingly, the exception was provided once more by Butler's Stores, which advertised its Lybro overalls without attempting to disguise their use in connection with manual work (Figure 3. *The Oxford Times* 28 February 1930). More in general, aside from the image of the undergraduate, much of Oxford retailers' advertising material, while benefiting from improved printing techniques, did not substantially differ from pre-war conventions. The imagery used did not seek to portray realistic figures, but rather ideal "types." The prospective buyer was presented with images of desirable, leisured, or

Figure 3
Butler's advert. *The Oxford Times* 28 February 1930. Reproduced by permission of the British Library, shelfm. 509 (Courtesy of Newsquest Oxfordshire Ltd).

even luxurious masculine lifestyles, or, more rarely, of obstacles overcome and success achieved, all through the wearing of a particular set of often inexpensive clothes. The power of these images lies in their inclusiveness. All Oxford men, except the very poorest—and car workers were not among these—could aspire to the images of manly elegance provided by shops such as the Fifty Shilling Tailors (Figure 4. *The Oxford Times* 28 September 1934).

Paradoxically, given the association made by many commentators between car workers and chain stores, the latter's appeal to a working-class clientele was far from explicit, although inexpensiveness was often emphasized: a Burton sale brochure, for example, announced that "really good clothes" had been reduced in price "and brought within the reach of every man's purse."[5] Also, although there is no definite evidence concerning the social status of Burton's customers (or, indeed, of other chain stores), Frank Mort has suggested that the evidence "points to men in subaltern social groups" (Mort 1996: 137). In 1930s Oxford, though, car workers were not necessarily the social group most strongly influenced by economic considerations in their choice of clothes. It is interesting to find undergraduates in 1935 furtively buying their flannel trousers from Marks & Spencer. According to one observer, "They were all skirmishing

Figure 4
Fifty Shilling Tailors advert. *The Oxford Times* 28 September 1934. Reproduced by permission of the British Library, shelfm. 1304 (Courtesy of Newsquest Oxfordshire Ltd).

to get to the cheap trousers. As soon as one had made his hasty purchase, another would dive out from behind the fancy goods and take his place" (*The Isis* 5 June 1935). By the 1930s, it was widely acknowledged that undergraduates' spending power was much reduced in comparison with earlier generations of students (*The Oxford Times* 4 December 1931). For many, then, making their purchases from cheap chain stores may have been a necessity. That such purchases were made furtively, though, seems to confirm the stores' relatively low social status.

The merchandise sold by stores such as Burton was not always necessarily acceptable for students. This is clearly reflected in the difficulties experienced by Ralph Glasser, an ex-presser in a Glasgow garment factory, who had won a scholarship to Oxford just before the outbreak of the Second World War. While sitting with other students in a study group, he observed that the others were mostly wearing "loose tweed jackets and flannel trousers . . . in varying shades of gray or dark blue, with cotton shirts and college ties; a few wore silk shirts in pastel shades and loosely knotted ties of Shantung silk in glowing colors." Glasser himself "felt staidly overdressed in my gray worsted suit, my only one, bought in Burtons for fifty shillings . . . before leaving Glasgow." Significantly, he planned to acquire "the uniform of tweed jacket and bags" as soon as he "dared spend more money" (Glasser 1988: 18).

While Glasser's own sartorial mistakes were made when attempting to enter a socially more privileged milieu, his scathing comments concerning the socialist and academic Richard Crossman indicate that such mistakes were not exclusive to social "climbers." Glasser compared the elegant gray suit and matching silk tie worn by Crossman for a seminar, with the "shabby flannels . . . tweed jacket with leather patches at the elbows, gray or dun shirt and red tie" that he had worn at Socialist meetings, and "which he must have thought gave him a proletarian appearance" (Glasser 1988: 18–19). In Glasser's opinion Crossman's style of dressing reflected his essential elitism and distance from the working class. It could, though, also reflect the impossibility of defining—and adopting—an accurate and distinctively "working-class" clothing style. It was certainly the case that Cowley car workers never acquired such easily recognizable symbols as undergraduates' flannel trousers or plus-fours.

It was mostly when rules were transgressed that it became clear that boundaries of "correct" dress did in fact exist. Among the workers at Morris Radiators, "dandies" stood out by wearing inappropriately genteel clothing to work, and subverting the distinction between everyday and Sunday clothes. One such "dandy" was a certain Raoul de Oscar-Thorpe, who according to a fellow worker, would always be seen with a walking stick, yellow gloves and a trilby hat; most importantly, he "came to work in them and all." Although he was a very good workman and obviously likeable, his style of clothing led to thinly disguised reservations in others' estimation: "He thought he was a gentleman . . . he was a proper show-off . . . Oh yes, a right dandy. I liked him though" (Exell 1978: 72).

* * *

Surveying the inter-war period, Robert Graves and Alan Hodge considered that while in the 1920s Oxford and Cambridge had been "two main hubs of advanced recreational fashion," by the 1930s they were reduced to the status of "merely suburbs of London" (Graves and Hodge 1995 [1940]: 122). Notions of suburbanization and of homogeneity, though, are not particularly helpful in examining men's apparel in 1930s Oxford. The main impetus behind men's choice of clothes seems to have been membership of a male group, however at times ill-defined: to some extent at least, consumption was embraced as a way of reinforcing collective masculine identities. Whether this means, though, that such identities had by the 1930s become "commercialized" is doubtful. Certainly, neither undergraduates nor car workers can easily be pigeon-holed as manipulated by retailers and advertisers; they seem rather to have co-existed in an uneasy relationship of mutual dependence and distrust.

The notion of the "modern" played an important, if ambiguous, role in male consumer discourses of this period. Critics of Oxford's development as an industrial center may have lamented the arrival of car workers as the shock troops of modernity. And yet it was the undergraduates, with their flannel trousers and plus-fours, who were by far the most highly visible symbols of the modern Oxford of the 1930s. The "timeless"—and still very influential—image of Oxford, of "stone wall retreats where flanneled youths play croquet amidst the oak and the elm" (Dougill 1998: 235) has in fact its origins in representations of the "modern," fashionable Oxford man of the inter-war years.

Notes

1. The population of Oxford had grown from 62,000 in 1911 to 97,000 in 1939. In 1911, about 27 per cent of adults had been engaged in some form of domestic service. Although unemployment reached 3,614 in September 1932, Oxford escaped the worst of the Depression.
2. "Smoothing the way . . .," Walters brochure, n.d., Oxford Trade 6, John Johnson Collection, Bodleian Library, University of Oxford.
3. "The Plough Inn," Austin Reed brochure, 1935, Oxford Trade 6, John Johnson Collection.
4. These incidents seem to have been more common in the 1920s than the 1930s, possibly as a reflection of the greater general conformity in dress (and possibly behavior) apparent in the later period.
5. "Record sale," Montague Burton brochure, n.d., Oxford Trade 6, John Johnson Collection.

References

Benson, J. 1994. *The Rise of Consumer Society in Britain 1880–1980*. London: Longman.

Betjeman, J. 1990 [1938]. *John Betjeman's Oxford*. Oxford: Oxford University Press.

Breazeale, K. 1994. "In Spite of Women: *Esquire* Magazine and the Construction of the Male Consumer." *Signs* 20: 1–22.

Breward, C. 1999. *The Hidden Consumer. Masculinities, Fashion and City Life 1860–1914*. Manchester: Manchester University Press.

Byrde, P. 1979. *The Male Image. Men's Fashion in Britain 1300–1970*. London: Batsford.

Chenoune, F. 1993. *A History of Men's Fashion*. Paris: Flammarion.

Cherwell, The 1930–1939.

Cole, D. H. and M. Cole. 1938. *Off With Her Head!* London: Collins.

Dataller, R. 1933. *A Pitman Looks at Oxford*. London: Dent.

Davies, A. 1992. *Leisure, Gender and Poverty. Working-Class Culture in Salford and Manchester, 1900–1939*. Buckingham: Open University Press.

De Marly, D. 1985. *Fashion for Men. An Illustrated History*. London: Batsford.

Dougill, J. E. 1998. *Oxford in English Literature. The Making and Undoing of "The English Athens."* Ann Arbor, MI: University of Michigan Press.

Elton, Lord. 1938. *Among Others*. London: Collins.

Exell, A. 1978. "Morris Motors in the 1930s." *History Workshop Journal* 6: 52–78.

Fasnacht, R. 1954. *A History of the City of Oxford*. Oxford: Basil Blackwell.

Fowler, D. 1992. "Teenage Consumers? Young Wage-earners and Leisure in Manchester, 1919–1939." In A. Davies and S. Fielding (eds), *Workers' Worlds: Cultures and Communities in Manchester and Salford, 1880–1939*, pp. 133–55. Manchester: Manchester University Press.

Glasser, R. 1988. *Gorbals Boy at Oxford*. London: Chatto & Windus.

Graves, R. and A. Hodge 1995 [1940]. *The Long Weekend. A Social History of Great Britain 1918–1939*. London: Abacus.

Greenfield, J., S. O'Connell and C. Read 1999. "Gender, Consumer Culture and the Middle-class Male." In A. Kidd and D. Nicholls (eds), *Gender, Civic Culture and Consumerism. Middle-class Identity in Britain, 1800–1940*, pp. 183–97. Manchester: Manchester University Press.

Gunn, S. 1999. "The Public Sphere, Modernity and Consumption: New Perspectives on the History of the English Middle-class." In A. Kidd and D. Nicholls (eds), *Gender, Civic Culture and Consumerism. Middle-class Identity in Britain, 1800–1940*, pp. 12–29. Manchester: Manchester University Press.

Isis, The 1930–1939.

Karaka, D. F. 1933. *The Pulse of Oxford*. London: Dent.

Levy, H. 1948. *The Shops of Britain. A Study of Retail Distribution*. London: Kegan Paul.

Light, A. 1991. *Forever England. Femininity, Literature and Conservatism between the Wars*. London: Routledge.

Maidment, B. 1998. "101 Things To Do with a Fantail Hat—Dustmen, Dirt, and Dandyism 1820–1860" (unpublished paper delivered at the "Work and the Image" conference, University of Leeds).

Marchand, R. 1985. *Advertising the American Dream. Making Way for Modernity, 1920–1940*. Berkeley, CA: University of California Press.

Morris, J. 1987 [1965]. *Oxford*. Oxford: Oxford University Press.

Mort, F. and P. Thompson 1994. "Retailing, Community Culture and Masculinity in 1950s Britain: The Case of Montague Burton, Tailor of Taste." *History Workshop Journal* 38: 106–27.

Mort, F. 1996. *Cultures of Consumption. Masculinities and Social Space in Late Twentieth-Century Britain*. London: Routledge.

Nystrom, P. H. 1928. *Economics of Fashion*. New York: The Ronald Press Co.

Orwell, G. 1965 [1937]. *The Road to Wigan Pier*. London: Heinemann Educational.

Oxford Mail 1930–1939.

Oxford Times, The 1930–1939.

Priestley, J. B. 1997 [1934]. *English Journey*. London: The Folio Society.

Richards, J. 1989 [1984]. *The Age of the Dream Palace. Cinema and Society in Britain 1930–1939*. London: Routledge.

Sennett, R. 1974. *The Fall of Public Man*. Cambridge: Cambridge University Press.

Sigsworth, E. M. 1990. *Montague Burton. The Tailor of Taste*. Manchester: Manchester University Press.

Sinclair, J. G. 1931. *Portrait of Oxford*. Sturry: Veracity Press.

Surman, P. 1992. *Pride of the Morning. An Oxford Childhood*. Stroud: Alan Sutton Publishing.

Thwaite, A. (ed.) 1986 [1976]. *My Oxford*. London: Robson Books.

Veblen, T. 1994 [1899]. *The Theory of the Leisure Class*. New York: Dover Publications.

Waugh, E. 1980 [1945]. *Brideshead Revisited*. London: Penguin Books.

Whiting, R. C. 1983. *The View from Cowley: The Impact of Industrialization upon Oxford, 1918–1939*. Oxford: Clarendon Press.

Willis, D. 1987. *Early Days in Oxford*. Oxford: The Amate Press.

Wilson, E. 1985. *Adorned in Dreams. Fashion and Modernity*. London: Virago.

Yee, C. 1944. *The Silent Traveler in Oxford*. London: Methuen & Co.

Fashion Theory, Volume 4, Issue 4, pp.447–466
Reprints available directly from the Publishers.
Photocopying permitted by licence only.

Fashioning the Playboy: Messages of Style and Masculinity in the Pages of *Playboy* Magazine, 1953–1963

Becky Conekin

Dr. Becky Conekin is a Research Fellow and Lecturer in Cultural and Historical Studies at the London College of Fashion. She is co-editor of *Moments of Modernity: Reconstructing Britain 1945–1964*, Rivers Oram/NYU Press, 1999 with Frank Mort and Chris Waters. The revised version of her 1998 Ph.D. in History from the University of Michigan will appear in 2001 as *"The Autobiography of a Nation:" The Festival of Britain, 1951, Representing Britain in the Post-war World,* Manchester University Press, distributed in the US by St. Martin's Press.

Many people believe that there were no general men's magazines, especially none with a marked interest in fashion, until the 1980s. According to Sean Nixon "advertising and publishing debates" raged in Britain "between 1983 and 1989" over how to produce a viable formula for general-interest men's magazines, which included some attention to the issue of masculine fashionability (Nixon 1996*:* 129).[1] On this debate, Nixon quotes Simon Marquis, amongst others, writing in 1985 in the advertising trade's "Bible," *Campaign*. There Marquis argued that a men's general-interest magazine would not work because:

> While women become "friends" with their magazines there is an inbuilt male resistance to the idea of a magazine that makes public

> and shares ideas about being a man. To men it is an unacceptable contradiction. Self-consciousness is permissible, even attractive in a women [*sic*]; it is perceived as weak and unmanly in a man (Marquis, as quoted by Nixon 1996: 129).

But, of course, beyond the narrower confines of the British publishing industry there were earlier examples of male magazines that addressed men publicly, sharing "ideas about being a man," often through recourse to debates on fashionable consumption. Examples include the inter-war *Esquire* and the early fifties *Modern Man*, but in the post-war period the most popular one was *Playboy*.[2] Barbara Ehrenreich asserts that *Playboy* "encouraged the sense of membership in a fraternity of male rebels" and its founder, Hugh Hefner, wrote in the first editorial: "We want to make clear from the very start, we aren't a 'family magazine.' If you're somebody's sister, wife or mother-in-law and picked us up by mistake, please pass us along to the man in your life and get back to your *Ladies' Home Companion*" (Ehrenreich 1983: 43). Ehrenreich has brilliantly shown how "*Playboy* was . . . like the party organ of a diffuse and swelling movement" which called for a new, single, heterosexual, consuming male, who escaped the trap of marriage or in her words: "the bondage of breadwinning" (Ehrenreich 1983: 42, 51). Building on Ehrenreich's argument, I am interested in how *Playboy* addressed, and thereby simultaneously helped to create, this new masculine, always (allegedly) heterosexual, consumer, especially in relation to clothes and fashion in its first decade. Ehrenreich goes so far as to argue that the nude female centerfolds were only included in *Playboy* to "protect it" from the charge of homosexuality—to make it "impervious to the ultimate sanction against male rebellion"—"queerness" (Ehrenreich 1983: 51). Whether or not we accept this radical account of *Playboy*'s agenda, we can certainly view the magazine, with its one million plus readers by its third year, as an important site in the construction of a particular form of masculinity—or perhaps, more accurately, particular forms of masculinities—known then as the "playboy," the "swinger" or the "hip bachelor."

Ehrenreich has shown how Hefner believed that by the end of its first decade *Playboy* even had the power to inspire men to work harder than they might otherwise. She quotes him as stating:

> ". . . Playboy exists, in part, as a motivation for men to expend greater effort in their work, develop their capabilities further and climb higher on the ladder of success." This kind of motivation, he went on, "is obviously desirable in our competitive, free enterprise system," apparently unaware that the average reader was more likely to be a white-collar "organization man" or blue-collar employee than a free entrepreneur himself (Ehrenreich 1983: 46).

Certainly, Ehrenreich is being ironic here, recognizing that Hefner was not "unaware" of his readers' socio-economic backgrounds, but actually more interested in creating the illusion and fantasy of a more upscale clientele for his magazine. Anxieties about the class status of its constituency were revealed in the first survey of *Playboy*'s readers, conducted by "an independent market research organization," Gould, Gleiss and Benn, Inc., and published in the September 1955 issue (*Playboy,* Vol. 2, No. 9: 36–7). There Hefner and the magazine announced that: "over 70% of *Playboy's* readers have attended college." But a closer look revealed that only 29.8% of readers had a college degree at the time of the survey, while 42.1% had attended college for "less than 4 years." Under the list marked with an asterisk the text read: "Over half of the 'College' group are students at the present time and a good percentage may be expected to join the 'College degree' group later" (*Playboy,* Vol. 2, No. 9: 36). "The great majority of *Playboy*'s readers are business and professional men and the young men in college who will be in business and the professions in two or three years. *Playboy* has a greater percentage of college men in its audience than any other national magazine (24.6%)" (*Playboy,* Vol. 2, No. 9: 36). Hefner clearly desired his readers to be perceived as "college-educated" whether they actually were or not. Categories such as "the college man" and "the professional" were actively promoted as models of a particular kind of aspirational, white, heterosexual, American male fashionability in this period, as opposed to the celebration of rougher, working-class masculinities found in Hollywood films such as *The Wild One* or *Rebel Without a Cause* (Votolato 1996: 245).[3]

Hefner also distinguishes the playboy as distinct from outdoor types who spent their leisure time shooting, hunting or fishing. In the very first issue in December 1953, along with the centerfold of Marilyn Monroe, Hugh Hefner gave his readers a sort of manifesto that asserted their masculine right to "spend[ing] most of our time inside . . . mixing up cocktails and an hors d'oeuvre or two, putting a little mood music on the phonograph and inviting in a female acquaintance for a quiet discussion on Picasso, Nietzsche, jazz, sex," rather than "thrashing through thorny thickets or splashing about in fast flowing streams" (*Playboy*, Vol. 1, No. 1: n.p.). *Playboy* defined its reader two years later as: "sophisticated, intelligent, urban—a young man-about-town, who enjoys good, gracious living" (*Playboy*, Vol. 2, No. 9: 36). The art historian, Christopher Reed, has argued that: "If the domestic is the main arena for the enforcement of conventional divisions of masculinity and femininity (along with their complement, heterosexuality), however, the modern home has also been a staging ground for rebellion against these norms" (Reed 1996: 16). The playboy's "bachelor pad," as represented implicitly and explicitly in the pages of the magazine, provides a perfect example of the reinforcement of heterosexuality and conventional masculinity and the simultaneous creation of more rebellious and allegedly liberated forms of both.

As Steven Cohan has written, *Playboy* magazine promulgated the fantasy of the "bachelor pad" in its 1956 series, with its alliterative title, "*Playboy*'s Penthouse Apartment: A High Handsome Haven for the

Bachelor in Town" (Cohan 1996). Cohan contends that: "The bachelor pad operated as a site of consumerism; it marked the single man's marginal position in relation to domestic ideology of the period, while at the same time allowing for his recuperation as a consumer whose masculinity could be redeemed—even glamorized—by the things he bought to accessorize his virility" (Cohan 1996: 28). What these imagined urban "playboys" were encouraged to consume in the realm of fashion is one of the main concerns of this article.

Playboy "Was Written and Edited for Hugh M. Hefner"

In a piece published in 1991, which was an attempt to revisit the girls' comics she had worked on more than ten years earlier, Angela McRobbie called for scholars to examine "production values" and the "ideas and values of those working on magazines" as a way to further understand magazines and their appeal to their audiences (McRobbie 1991: 186).[4] McRobbie's challenge is a good one, especially in relation to *Playboy*. It is difficult fully to understand *Playboy* without considering the character of its creator and editor. This may not always be the case with every text, but Hefner is famous for exercising extraordinary control over all aspects of *Playboy*. That, along with the fact that the magazine was in every way a dream come true for its founder, suggests that some biographical information will shed light on the curious creation that was *Playboy* in its first decade. An early editor, Jack Kessie, has stated that: "That magazine was written and edited for Hugh M. Hefner" (Kessie, as quoted by Halberstam 1993: 574). So, who was this Hefner in the early fifties?

Hefner had graduated from high school in a Chicago suburb in 1944, where he was more renowned for his extra-curricular than his academic pursuits. He had been raised in a Methodist household that permitted neither smoking nor drinking and observed the Sabbath so seriously that not even the radio was played. After graduating, he volunteered for the army, but his war duty consisted of working as a typing clerk in Camp Hood, Texas. One biographer reports that Hefner "found the language and behavior of the military profoundly shocking. For a boy who had only just turned 18, never swore, was a virgin, the infantry came as an exceedingly nasty surprise" (Miller 1984: 27). In the spring of 1946 he returned to Illinois and his girlfriend Mildred Williams, whom he married three years later. He enrolled at the University of Illinois, Urbana through the GI Bill, joining his girlfriend, who was already studying to be a teacher. Hefner hoped to be a journalist, but majored in Psychology. He also picked up on his high school pursuits, contributing cartoons to the university daily newspaper and acting as managing editor of a campus magazine called *The Shaft*. In 1948 he wrote an enthusiastic review of the Kinsey Report for *The Shaft*, in which he expressed his disdain for the hypocrisy of American public attitudes towards sex. The ground-breaking Kinsey Report indicated that 86 per cent of American men had premarital sex, 70 per cent had sex with prostitutes and 40 per cent engaged in extra marital intercourse. From that moment on it seems that Hefner decided that sex was a legitimate area of scholarship, and he began to read everything from medical journals to pornography in the name of such academic study (Miller, 1984: 28–9).[5] (In the first issue of *Playboy* the introductory text states: "We believe, too, that we are filling a publishing need only slightly less important than the one just taken care of by the Kinsey Report" (*Playboy*, Vol. 1, No. 1: n.p.)

He graduated from the University of Illinois in 1949 and applied unsuccessfully to every magazine and newspaper in Chicago. After a brief stint in the personnel department of a carton company, Hefner entered a Master's program in Sociology at Northwestern University on Chicago's North shore. He and his wife were living with his parents and she was teaching school. Hefner only lasted one semester in graduate school. However, while he was at Northwestern he built on his new-found cause, writing a paper on "Sex Behavior and the US Law" in which he argued that a complete re-examination of all laws relating to sex was necessary (Miller 1984: 31). Next, he held the post of advertising copywriter for a large Chicago department store before moving to *Esquire* as a promotional copywriter. According to one biographer, Russell Miller, *Esquire* was Hefner's favorite magazine and he was "thrilled" to get the job (Miller 1984: 32). In late 1951 *Esquire* moved their headquarters to New York and Hefner decided not to follow. Nevertheless, his employment at *Esquire* left a lasting impact. It explains the seemingly odd, frequent comparisons between that magazine and *Playboy* that appeared in the first few volumes of Hefner's creation (see, for example, *Playboy*, Vol. 1, No. 5, April 1954: 3). In 1957 when *Playboy*'s circulation figures were closing in on *Esquire*'s—the January issue of *Playboy* sold 687,593 copies, while *Esquire*'s sold 778,190—Hefner is featured in a series of photographic cartoons as sitting at a desk, and the caption reads: "I'm truly sorry Mr. Smart [then publisher of *Esquire*] but at present our staff is at full capacity. Leave your name with the office boy and I'll call if something comes up" (Miller 1984: 59).

The story of *Esquire* is an interesting one, and it highlights the centrality of style and fashion to Hefner's conception of *Playboy*.[6] In 1933 the editorial team who had founded *Apparel Arts*, "the first male fashion magazine aimed at trade people, manufacturers, wholesalers and retailers," launched *Esquire* "in the same spirit . . . at the general public" (Chenoune 1993: 188). Subscriptions to *Esquire* reached 728,000 by 1937. The man behind both magazines, Arnold Gingrich, was determined "to liberate male stylishness from the closed little circle of 'high society' with its English traditions, its private schools, clubs and shopping trips to London" (ibid.). Gingrich pitched *Esquire* at the middle-class male consumer, attempting "to democratize the game of fashion and stylishness" (ibid.). Its broader-based constituency distinguishes this phenomenon from earlier examples of masculine representations built around conspicuous consumption, such as those outlined by Christopher Breward for late Victorian Britain and Paula Fass for 1920s America (Breward 1999; Fass 1977). In addition, Gingrich's magazines were promoting ready-to-wear, not custom-made, clothing, which the American industry was perfectly placed to provide, as it entered "a golden age that would last until the mid-1960s" (Chenoune 1993: 188).

Miller claims that Hefner saw *Esquire* as "the arbiter of taste and style, the very last word in male sophistication. He had bought it for years whenever he could afford it, read it with admiration, laughed at the cartoons and spent many happy hours studying the lustrous girls drawn by Alberto Vargas and George Petty" (Miller 1984: 32). By the forties, in addition to being the most fashionable, *Esquire* was also the most daring men's magazine, with several issues declared obscene by the US Post Office. But by the time Hefner joined its staff its editors had begun what they called the "rescue of *Esquire* from bawditry" (Miller 1984: 33). Hefner had been disappointed by this turn of events, finding even the forties version of *Esquire* less bawdy than he would have liked. In 1952, in the fifty-second volume of what he called his *Comic Autobiography*, which he had been writing since high school, Hefner admitted: "I'd like to produce an entertainment magazine for the city-bred guy—breezy, sophisticated. The girlie features would guarantee the initial sale, but the magazine would have quality too" (Hefner 1952, as quoted by Miller 1984: 36). A work colleague from about this time, Vince Tajiri, says he remembers Hefner talking "a lot about becoming a publisher himself, but I don't think anyone took much notice. I thought he was very immature for his age. He was totally unsophisticated, but he had an obsession with sex" (Tajiri, as quoted by Miller 1984: 35). Such a characterization of Hugh Hefner appears repeatedly in the reminiscences of people who knew him just prior to and in the early days of *Playboy*.

Having finally moved from his parents' house to a five-room apartment in Hyde Park on the South side of Chicago, Hefner was next employed as circulation manager for *Children's Activities* magazine, running their direct-mail subscription campaign, which taught him valuable lessons in how to distribute a national title. He and a college friend began working in the evenings on the mock-up of a magazine they initially called *Stag Party*. Hefner explained that the idea was a magazine based on the "contemporary equivalent of wine, women and song, although not necessarily in that order" (Miller 1984: 37). He was able to borrow a little money from a bank and a little more from a loan company, and then he hocked the contemporary living-room furniture that he had bought with money borrowed from his parents. Ray Russell, a writer and editor who worked for *Playboy* in the fifties, has said that: "A lot of it was good luck, random choice, being carried on the tide of the times . . . It was a matter of being the right magazine able to take advantage of a rising economy, more than any degree of conscious planning" (Russell, as quoted by Halberstam 1993: 573–4). The prime example of Hefner's good luck and being in the right place at the right time is that in 1952 he discovered in a trade publication that the famous semi-nude Marilyn Monroe calendar had been printed by a company in Chicago. Hefner went directly the same morning to see that company, the John Baumgarth Company. Because of the fear of prosecution for obscenity, Baumgarth did not believe he could use the pictures of Monroe any more than he had, which consisted of featuring them in a free promotional calendar to be used by garages and similar clients. He agreed to sell Hefner the rights to publish the Monroe semi-nude pictures and threw in the color separations for a fee of $500 (Miller 1984: 37–8). At that moment Hefner knew he had the key to a winning first issue; in December 1953 Volume One, Issue One appeared on the news-stands.

Hefner's Fashion and Consumer Choices

David Halberstam, in his best-selling work on fifties America, has argued that "Hefner's great strength was his lack of sophistication. If he was square, he still longed to share the better world, which was now increasingly available around him; in that he mirrored the longings of millions of young men of similar background, more affluent than their parents, wanting a better and freer life" (Halberstam 1993: 574). Hefner shared other heterosexual, newly college-educated, veterans' fantasies of a life with fewer strings and more pleasure. His subscription pitch in the April 1956 issue of *Playboy* defined "a playboy" in terms of happiness, taste and pleasure. It ran:

> What is a playboy? Is he simply a wastrel, a ne'er-do-well, a fashionable bum? Far from it. He can be a sharp minded young business executive, a worker in the arts, a university professor, an architect or an engineer. He can be many things, provided he possesses a certain kind of view. He must see life not as a vale of tears, but as a happy time, he must take joy in his work, without regarding it as the end of all living; he must be an alert man, a man of taste, a man sensitive to pleasure, a man who—without acquiring the stigma of voluptuary or dilettante—can live life to the hilt. This is the sort of man we mean when we use the word playboy (*Playboy*, Vol. 2, No. 4: n.p.).

A little over a year later Hefner described himself and his pleasures in *Playboy*. Here we can see both how *Playboy* was produced by and for Hefner, and what sort of fashions and commodities were necessary for "the playboy" lifestyle. In the June 1957 issue Hefner wrote of himself:

> His dress is conservative and casual. He always wears loafers . . . There is an electronic entertainment wall in his office, very much like the one featured in *Playboy*'s Penthouse apartment, that includes hi-fi, AM-FM radio, tape and television, and will store up to 2000

> LPs . . . He likes jazz, foreign films, Ivy League clothes, gin and tonic and pretty girls—the same sort of things the *Playboy* readers like—and his approach to life is as fresh, sophisticated, and yet admittedly sentimental as is the magazine (*Playboy,* Vol. 4, No. 6: n.p.).

According to his biographers, however, Hefner's dress style had not always been "casual and conservative" or Ivy-inspired, as he also called it in *Playboy*. It is reported that in the first year or so of *Playboy*, Hefner sported white socks and "zoot suits" with his penny loafers. It was the chance encounter with Victor Lownes III, whom Hefner immediately made editor in charge of promotion and advertising, that transformed his style. Lownes's "Ivy League look" inspired Hefner to change his own (Miller 1984: 64).

The original zoot suits were, of course, worn by stylish African American musicians in the 1930s. But, they came to be the basis of many an American man's look in the forties and even gave rise to the "bold look" promoted by the fashion industry in 1947 (Chenoune, 1993: 208). This was probably the sort of suit Hefner was wearing in the early fifties, a watered-down version of a zoot suit. Yet this still carried some connotations of rebellion and blackness—two associations he was shedding when he donned his Ivy League look. According to the fashion historian Farid Chenoune, both Oxbridge and the Ivy League were thought of as sites of new male fashion trends in the inter-war period (Chenoune 1993: 156). But, twenty or more years later, the smart-casual look of button-downs, blazers, slacks and loafers could be called conservative. Although an advocate of African American jazz, both personally and in the pages of *Playboy*, and later a truly equal-opportunity employer in his international Playboy Clubs, Hefner's fashion choices for himself and for his readers were decidedly WASP-ish. They eschewed not only any African American references, but also any hint of the working class. Neither the popular fifties clothing code for youthful rebellion—tee shirt, blue jeans and black leather jacket—nor the bohemian Village look of the Beats ever found its way into the world of *Playboy* (Chenoune 1993).[7]

Hefner had by 1954, it seems, a very clear idea of both what he and his readership should look like. The youthfulness of their attire should be represented by their relative casualness, not their rebelliousness. They should not look stuffy or dated, like their fathers, but "fresh and sophisticated" in their Ivy League clothes. As Jo Barraclough Paoletti has shown for turn-of-the-century American men's fashion, younger men have often distinguished themselves from older men through their clothes choices (Paoletti 1985). Pumphrey has written specifically of how older men in the fifties and sixties displayed "an aggressive indifference to dress and a silent avoidance of bodily display," "refusing to take notice of fashion" (Pumphrey, as cited by Craik 1993: 191).

Hefner certainly believed that generational differences were key. In his second installment of his "Playboy Philosophy" in January 1963, he claimed that there was a new, positive generation who "searched for new answers and new opportunities." Although *Life* magazine had dubbed this group "The Takeover Generation" the previous autumn, Hefner thought his name, "The Upbeat Generation", was more apt. Simultaneously revealing his personal sense of American history, Hefner (1963) explained that: "Actually, the spirit and attitude of the Upbeats is right out of the first part of this century—it's the same optimistic viewpoint and zest for living that made America great in the first place. In the 1930s and 1940s we lost faith in ourselves, we hid our individual identities in groups . . ." (*Playboy,* Vol. 10, No. 1: 50). But, according to Hefner, this new generation of the early sixties was "bringing this country alive again" (ibid.). He was explicit that this "Upbeat Generation"—"the only hope America has for the future"—did not consist of real radicals or revolutionaries. They were not the "part of this new generation [who] rejected the old in a negative way, simply turning their backs on society and ceasing to communicate" (ibid.). No, the men who subscribed to *Playboy* were those going to university, heading for decent jobs and moving up the social ladder.

Texts on *Playboy*

Curiously, given *Playboy's* huge popularity at the time—the first issue in 1953 exceeded expectations, selling 53,991 copies, one year later circulation was 175,000 and by 1956 it had passed the one million mark—it has only seldom been looked at seriously by scholars (Ehrenreich 1983: 42; Dines 1995: 257). And when it has been, writers and scholars have most often used *Playboy* to illustrate a larger point about for instance, feminism, in Barbara Ehrenreich's case, or "queer masculinity" in Steven Cohan's (Ehrenreich 1983: 42–5; Cohan 1996: 28–41). But what happens if we refocus and examine *Playboy* more in the way we might a woman's magazine? Such a re-examination of *Playboy* in no way disagrees or detracts from those other angles; it is merely an attempt to set out different parameters for this influential magazine. Cultural studies scholarship on girls and women's magazines has generally focused on questions of fantasy, desire and aspiration (White 1970; Winship 1987; Wilson 1985; Walkerdine 1990; McRobbie 1991; Craik 1993). Such are the realms of the current argument regarding *Playboy.*

In these terms the most relevant scholarly article on *Playboy* is by Gail Dines, who looks at the magazine in terms of what she calls "the sexualization of consumerism" (Dines 1995: 254–62). According to Dines, "'soft porn' or 'men's entertainment'" magazines "offer a 'lifestyle' that involves the consumption of numerous upmarket commodities as a way of capturing the ultimate prized commodity: lots and lots of attractive, young, big-breasted women, just like the ones masturbated to in the centerfold" (Dines 1995: 254). She further argues that: "As with all advertising, the actual product on offer was not the commodity being advertised but rather the fantasy of transformation this product promised to bring to the consumer's life . . . the pages of *Playboy* and *Penthouse* are filled with advertisements from companies such as Seagrams, Bensons and Hedges, Mercedes, Sony and Bugle Boy—a sign of both their upscale readership and mainstream status" (ibid.).

First doubts about Dine's interesting argument arise from reading the early issues of *Playboy*, which she herself states have been her focus (Dines 1995: 256). The editorial in Volume One, Issue Twelve, for instance, announced that *Playboy* would soon be "opening its pages" to advertisers. In the editorial Hefner explained that advertising was not included in *Playboy*'s first year of publication because the editors wanted "to first create a truly new and distinctive men's magazine" (*Playboy*, Vol. 1, No. 12: 3). Others have written that actually advertisers were quite cautious of appearing in *Playboy* initially, since it was not clear that the US Postal Service would allow such pornographic material to be delivered, much less what the public response would be (see, for example, Miller 1984: 64). But, for whatever reason, there was no advertising in the first twelve issues of *Playboy.* Furthermore, in its first few years the advertising was modest and sketchy, and it certainly does not include companies of the caliber of those listed by Dines. Most frequent were advertisements for mail-order "show-off" record racks, "tastefully designed drinkware with an authentic black and gold coin collection ringing the top of the glasses," and an ash tray shaped like a golf club "ready to whack one down the fairway" (*Playboy,* Vol. 2, No. 10: 57, 61).

On a wider level, although Dines seems to be making an anti-reductionist argument about *Playboy*, her reading still contains a certain literalism that makes the beautiful, semi-clad woman the *telos* of male consumption. Such a reading underestimates the overall aspirational character of *Playboy* magazine. Yes, of course, it was a "girlie" magazine, and women's bodies were clearly commodified therein. However, the other commodities presented in what she calls the "'service' features on the latest upmarket consumer products" were not only laid out as a means to an end; they were also a large part of the goal. Dines has truly undervalued the importance of those other "prizes," especially for the upwardly mobile, lower-middle-class male in fifties and early sixties America. Moreover, it is surely naïve to argue that advertisements in particular periodicals correspond or even map simply on to their readers' socio-economic status. Does anyone really believe that the majority of women who read fashion magazines can afford to buy designer clothes, for example? Such magazines are the stuff of fantasy, desire and aspiration: "fashion acts as a vehicle for fantasy," in Elizabeth Wilson's words (Wilson 1985: 246; see also, Craik 1993: 50–1). Many of the heterosexual male readers of *Playboy* would have served in the Second Word War and/or Korea, and then returned to a newly affluent and increasingly domesticated America, which was rife with and then recovering from McCarthyism. The *Playboy* readers were ready to move from military control and uniforms to personal choice in actions and dress. But, since many had been out of the dressing game for some time and most were attempting to move quickly and quietly up the social ladder, these men would have been happy to find a sexy monthly publication to guide their choices, as well as fuel their fantasies. A magazine that assumed these men had already climbed that ladder—that they owned expensive cars, boats, and apartments, read "the classics," knew how to cook, how to dress like East Coast, privately-educated men, how to select wine and liquor, etc.—would have had great appeal. Such a magazine, as many women and girls know, gives you the sense in the act of interpolating you as a reader that you would know how to do all those things once the opportunity arises. Halberstam has written that:

> *Playboy* shepherded a generation of young men to the good life. It helped explain how to buy a sports car, what kind of hi-fi set to buy, how to order in a restaurant, what kind of wine to drink with what kind of meal. For men whose parents had not gone to college, *Playboy* served a valuable function: It provided an early and elementary tutorial on the new American life-style. For those fearful of headwaiters in fancy restaurants, wary of slick salesmen in stores and of foreign-car dealers who seemed to speak a language never heard in Detroit, *Playboy* provided a valuable consumer service: It midwifed the readers into a world of increasing plenty (Halberstam 1993: 575–6).

But, here too, we must beware of literalism. Surely, it is more realistic to say that *Playboy* provided its readers with the satisfaction of thinking that if their dreams came true, they would know how to buy a foreign sportscar or order in an exclusive restaurant.

Barbara Ehrenreich writes of how, in mid-fifties America, Americans were encouraged to enjoy "a life of pleasurable consumption" and "fun morality" (Ehrenreich 1983: 46). She quotes the motivational researcher, Dr. Ernest Dichter, who told businessmen at the time: "We are now confronted with the problem of permitting the average American to feel moral . . . even when he is spending, even when he is not saving . . . One of the basic problems of prosperity, then is to demonstrate that the hedonistic approach to his life is a moral, not an immoral one" (Dichter, as quoted by Ehrenreich, 1983: 45). It is clear that *Playboy* was an early proponent of such "fun morality." The magazine did "offer a lifestyle" (not to mention an ideology), as Dines has argued. This was a lifestyle which "swung" not simply because it encouraged single, heterosexual men to stay single *and* be sexual, but also because it advocated fun through consumption. *Playboy*'s pages were filled with new goods, foods, drink and travel. Included in these new masculine, bachelor purchasing pleasures was the pleasure of shopping for clothes and accessories for himself. If we turn to the fashion and style pages of *Playboy* magazine in its first decade in existence, what do we find?

The Fashion and Style Pages of Early *Playboy*

We know from the work of Frank Mort that, by the mid-fifties, British mid-market menswear retailers had begun to address "a fashion-conscious, young adult man," and that this "resulted in a proliferation of styles" (Mort 1996: 140, 142). In many ways the fantasy of the American playboy provided a prototype for the British equivalent. At least as presented in the feature on *Playboy*'s "bachelor pad" in 1956, the American single male consumer was assumed already to own: "winter wear, summer wear, sports clothes, dress clothes . . . terry-cloth robes . . . flat-lying sweaters and knit T-shirts" (*Playboy*, Vol. 3, No. 10: 70; also reprinted with Cohan, 1996: 63–7). But the playboy needed assistance in choosing the right components for his copious wardrobe.

In *Playboy*'s first decade there was a marked shift in the tone of its fashion pages from didacticism to fantasy. The first fashion editor listed on *Playboy*'s masthead was Blake Rutherford. This Ivy League-inspired pseudonym belonged to Jack Kessie, who had contributed a freelance piece to the January 1955 issue, and then "was hired as an associate editor at $100 a week partly because Hefner liked the way he looked," according to Miller. Kessie was a graduate of Drake University in Des Moines, Iowa, and "he had the kind of casual elegance which Hefner thought exemplified the *Playboy* style" (Miller 1984: 67). As early as the January 1955 issue, Kessie's article, "The Well Dressed Playboy: *Playboy*'s Position on the Proper Male Attire," was accompanied by the byline: "Jack J. Kessie, *Playboy*'s apparel editor" (*Playboy,* Vol. 2, No. 2: 39). The tone of Kessie's articles, on style, fashion and accessories, whether written under the name of Kessie or Rutherford, was didactic. For example, in that first piece he started by acknowledging men's confusion over fashion choices:

> Although style changes in the men's fashion world are neither as dramatic nor as frequent as those enjoyed by the female, proper masculine dress can become a very confusing matter. If a man is concerned with how he looks, and he should be, he may find himself caught up in a perplexing, phantasmagoria of color combinations, patterns, styles, designs, fabrics and cuts (*Playboy*, Vol. 2, No. 2: 39).

Kessie's answer to the bewilderment of his readers was a vision of conservative, elegant, establishment dressing. References to conservatism were repeated again and again in his articles. For example, in the piece on the "The Well Dressed Man" Kessie explained: "Conservative in all departments we lean heavily towards those distinctive details of styling that point up the man as being *quietly* well dressed."[8] "His business shirts are of three basic collar styles, button-down, round (worn with safety pin) and tab . . . The Edwardian waistcoat is welcomed by our conservative man as an item of rare distinction . . . His hosiery follows the solid color line . . . The final mark of our well-tailored man dictates that his shoes be correctly coordinated to the rest of his apparel" (*Playboy*, Vol. 2, No. 2: 39). And such references to Englishness as the mark of conservatism were far from rare. Actual English ties and hats were advocated by Kessie, but even when writing about black dinner jackets and tailcoats he established a long link with Englishness. In "Formal Forecast: The Return to Black" "Blake Rutherford" announced to the playboys that:

> After a brief excursion into gaudier evening plumage last winter, the cocks of the walk who know their formal fashion are reverting to black, and depending on the niceties of fabric, tailoring and accessories to point up their individuality.
>
> Now we said black. Not midnight blue, not maroon, not burnt ochre. Just black. Black looks and feels right for all formal occasions, which is why it has been firmly entrenched among the knowledgeable for nearly 100 years, ever since an inconsolable Queen Victoria prescribed mourning for her court after the death of Albert. We recommend wearing it today for the very good reason that dramatic black, coupled with the tasteful crispness of white, lends an elegance of uniformity to dress-up affairs that no color can match (*Playboy,* Vol. 5, No. 1: 61–2).

"An elegance of uniformity" was what Kessie generally advocated in his autocratic tone. He claimed that there were ". . . certain basic tenets of style and cut in men's clothing that are unchangeable" (*Playboy*, Vol. 2, No. 9: 27). The key to that conservative message, not surprisingly given his own and Hefner's fashion choices, was summed up in two words: Ivy League. Be the article about "Summa Cum Style" (*Playboy*, Vol. 2, No. 10: 18) or "Ivy Action: The Right Look for the Beach, Boating, Tennis and the Links" (*Playboy*, Vol. 4, No 7: 20), Kessie recommended that the old East Coast, private universities held the answer to the playboy's style quandaries. According to Kessie, ". . . few will argue [in the Autumn of 1955] against the fact that it is to the Ivy Leaguers that we owe the current national acceptance of the trim, tapered, natural look in men's clothing" (*Playboy*, Vol. 2, No. 10: 18). This look included: a couple of blazers, complete with university crest, if you liked, a sports waistcoat, a "duffer" coat or double-breasted greatcoat, a crew neck long sleeve pullover, and a muffler either in cashmere, your "eastern club or midwestern fraternity" colors or "an authentic tartan plaid woven in Scotland by the very same fellow (Cambridge '07) who makes them for the British Royal Family" (ibid.). In a later article Kessie argued that "there is, believe it or not, an authentic Ivy look in active sportswear, just as there is in town"

(*Playboy*, Vol. 4, No. 7: 20). He told his readers to eschew "the kind of gruesome garbage . . . touted as the hottest news from Majorca, the Italian Riviera, Cap d'Antibes and Southern California: Old Testament sandals, ballet-dancer shirts that tie north of the navel, too-short swim trunk laced and latticed up the side, etc . . ." (ibid.). Instead, proper playboys should choose white shorts and shoes for tennis, teamed with a red imported French Lacoste knit shirt, for swimming, "trim, fly-front cotton poplin trunks with side-tabs for waist-clinching fit," and for golf, pleatless, poplin, olive green shorts, worn with "a good-looking glen, plaid, long sleeved shirt," and "the best golf shoes you can afford" (ibid.). For boating, Kessie believed the "Ivy-bred style" consisted of tan slacks from Kenya cloth, a long sleeve "marine blue sweater-shirt from Allen Solly, London," and "an additional husky shetland sweater or a short, zip-up jacket." "Blue Topsiders are *de rigueur* on deck," stated Kessie in his signature alliterative style (ibid.).

In all Kessie's fashion articles there was an implied promise. Dressing "properly" in the conservative, Ivy-inspired style meant that you were a playboy and as such you were destined for a more successful life at work, as well as in bed. When Kessie wasn't imagining his readers ensconced in Ivy League eating clubs, he envisioned them as "Madison Avenue advertising executives" (*Playboy*, Vol. 2, No. 5: 27), or "downtown brokers" (*Playboy,* Vol. 2, No. 9: 28). Acquiring the necessary marks of distinction was never going to be easy, but with sufficient effort, the transformation would become a natural part of the playboy's personality. As Kessie put it in "The Marks of the Well-Dressed Man":

> As you should know by this time, had you been following these columns zealously, being well-appointed is not a hit-or-miss proposition. It is a carefully planned strategem [*sic*] involving a broad view and a close watch on details. But once mastered, it is a process that becomes as effortless (and rewarding) as sampling 20-year-old Armagnac from a snifter (*Playboy,* Vol. 4, No. 3: 47).

The perfect blazer and the vintage Armagnac merged into a seamless *habitus*—an image of perfect taste, naturally acquired through a process of aging. Nobody need know how recently the playboy had come by these marks of distinction.

The clothing essentials recommended as "Marks of the Well-Dressed Man" were: a snap-brimmed hat, button-down shirts in white, yellow, blue, and brown and red with white, a suit made of fabric not with "too bold pattern, too hairy tweed, too nubby or shiny material," a tie featuring "restrained paisleys, stripes and all-over designs in warm pleasant colors," and fine Italian boots (*Playboy,* Vol. 4, No. 3: 69). But, as *Playboy* frequently reminded its readers in the early issues, "however well you select your head-to-toe garb, though, you'll still look like a bum or a bumpkin if you wear it—and treat it—badly" (*Playboy,* Vol. 4, No. 3:

70). Like the didactic literature it was, Kessie's article quoted a letter from Lord Chesterfield ("of overcoat and cigarette fame") to his son as "sage advice." He claimed Chesterfield had written: "Take good care always to be dressed like the reasonable people of your own age in the place where you are; whose dress is never spoken of one way or another, as either too negligent or too much studied" (ibid.). When put into a context more appropriate for business, Hefner's conservative, elegant style was advocated for all the other playboys.

Kessie's conservatism seemed to strike the appropriate note with *Playboy* readers. He generated numerous letters to the editor, some chastising him for omitting a tuxedo and dinner jacket from his *Basic Wardrobe*. "What self respecting playboy would be caught dead without a tuxedo and dinner jacket? Why it's almost as bad as finding a Madison Avenue ad-exec without a button-down shirt," wrote Martin Silver of Wantagh, New York (*Playboy*, Vol. 2, No. 12: 3). And more than one reader requested specific store advice on where to buy "Jack Kessie's 'Featherweights for Spring'" suits, which could be purchased for $26.50 at Brooks Brothers in New York or Chicago or at that famous department store in Chicago, Marshall Field's, in their "Young Chicagoan" shop (*Playboy*, Vol. 2, No. 8: 4).

However, by 1959 *Playboy* and its readers were assumed to have grown up in some ways. The sorts of fashion features typically targeted at female teenagers, which dictated the constitutive components of an appropriate wardrobe and reminded readers about the importance of repairing and maintaining their clothes and shoes, were now superseded by articles suffused with fantasies of wealth, luxury and travel. No longer was the *Playboy* reader to be told to polish his shoes. Under the magazine's first fashion director, Robert L. Green, the playboy was encouraged to imagine himself in the perfect "wardrobe for a jet weekend" to Paris and London, the "right raiment" at the country or yacht club, and the correct "sports car fashions," donned for Nassau Speed Week (*Playboy,* Vol. 6, No. 5: 38–9; *Playboy*, Vol. 7, No. 4: 37–8, 101; *Playboy*, Vol. 6, No. 4: 28–30, 89). Just as in upmarket women's fashion magazines, in *Playboy*'s late fifties and early sixties style pages the practical was shunned in favor of the fanciful and aspirational. By the end of the fifties the magazine had clearly established itself and its playboy lifestyle firmly enough to move into this other arena of fashion publishing. And although the length and content of the articles changed in the ensuing decades, *Playboy* never really looked back from this formula.[9]

Conclusion

The American historian Elaine Tyler May has argued in her book, *Homeward Bound,* that the post-war, Cold War ideology of containment extended to the home, where all sorts of sexualities were to be contained within the domestic dyad of the heterosexual, married couple (May 1988). *Playboy* magazine claimed that it contained the urban, sophisticated, heterosexual man's life. But, as with all magazines, what it really contained was heterosexual men's fantasies, their longings and their desires in post-war America. This was especially true for men like its founder, Hugh Hefner, who had gone to university on the GI Bill and who aimed to achieve more than their parents had in terms of material comforts, as well as sexual experiences. Hefner believed that, if you worked hard, you should be able to play hard, and that heterosexual sex should be a part of that. His long-time executive editor, Arthur Kretchmer, believes that: "Hefner helped the world to discover toys. He said 'Play, it's okay to play'" (Kretchmer, as quoted by Halberstam 1993: 576). This is a very generous reading of *Playboy.* A less generous one would argue that *Playboy* helped to contain the fantasies of men who had fought in US wars and returned home to a country with an extremely circumscribed version of heterosexual, domestic bliss and upward mobility, channeling their discontent and longings into tasteful luxury consumption.

In doing so it contradicted the widely held belief that such publications were profoundly gendered. It has been said that women's magazines claim to contain all aspects of women's lives, while magazines for men address them in terms of their interests—sports, hobbies, cars, etc. Men's lives cannot be contained within the pages of a single magazine, the argument runs.[10] As we saw at the beginning of this article, some editors and publishers began to question this in the mid-1980s. But, as this article has shown, Hefner's *Playboy* magazine achieved this end thirty years earlier. In the sixth issue, for example, a subscription advertisement defined *Playboy* as "the new entertainment magazine for men," "edited in the belief that men deserve a magazine of their own, and that such a publication should, properly, devote itself to the real interests of its audience." Detailing who it considered its audience, the advertisement explained: "Beyond that, *Playboy* is specifically styled to the tastes of the city-bred man—the man-about-town—the fellow concerned with proper dress, food and drink, art, literature (of the lighter sort, primarily) and, of course, women" (*Playboy,* Vol. 1, No. 6: n.p.). The British socialist and cultural critic, Judith Williamson, contends that for consumers commodities are, in addition to "congealed labor," also "congealed longing, the final form of an active wish" (Williamson 1988: 12). She asserts that: "The need for change, the sense that there must be something else, something different from the way things are, becomes the need for a new purchase . . . Consuming products does give a thrill, a sense of both belonging and being different, charging normality with the excitement of the unusual . . ." (Williamson, 1988: 12–13). One can hardly ask for a more apt description of early *Playboy*'s agenda. Its fashion pages advocated distinction through careful attention to detail, offering the possibility of combining conservatism in dress, success at work, and a new and exciting lifestyle in the realm of leisure. Especially in its first six years, under the tutelage of Jack Kessie, the playboy was assured that if he learned the lessons of how to dress in the Ivy League style, "like the reasonable people of your own age in the place where you are," his life would be enriched and he would be capable of moving easily up the social ladder (*Playboy*, Vol. 4, No. 3: 70). *Playboy* encouraged men in the fifties and sixties to charge their normal working lives with "the excitement of the unusual" through a unique, balanced combination of *risqué* images of beautiful women and conservative fashions.

Notes

1. Frank Mort, in his *Cultures of Consumption* (London: Routledge, 1996: 18), briefly discusses *Man About Town*, established in 1953.
2. To be fair, I should acknowledge that Nixon explains that publishers believed that the "'soft porn' magazine market was not the same as the 'general interest men's magazine' market" (Nixon 1996: 129). But, as I hope to show in this article, and as Barbara Ehrenreich has illustrated in *The Hearts of Men* (New York: Anchor Press, Doubleday, 1983: 42–51) in some very important ways, especially relevant to the 1950s and 1960s, *Playboy* magazine was much more than a soft porn magazine.
3. According to Kidwell, from the 1930s the American retailer and mail order catalogue, Sears, had defined their male customers as fitting into one of four groups: "the 'snappy' dresser with jazzy styling, the 'university', or fashion conscious young man, the 'business' man and the 'conservative'" (Kidwell and Steele 1989: 141.) On the mutually reinforcing representations of whiteness and heterosexuality, see Richard Dyer, *White* (1997). There he argues that ". . . there is implicit racial resonance to the idea, endemic in the representation of white heterosexuality, of sexual desire as itself dark . . ." (1997: 13). It seems that in the first decade of *Playboy*, at least, its images of masculinity generally excluded men of color, as well as working-class men. And, following from Dyer, we can assume that—consciously or unconsciously—it did this to shore up its claims of an exclusively heterosexual readership.
4. In this piece McRobbie also acknowledges the importance of a more reader-centered approach, which she includes and which was already being pursued by people like Janice Radway, Cora Kaplan, David Morley and Charlotte Brunsdon in their work on books, television and film. It was my original plan to interview some older men about the role of *Playboy* in their lives, and especially in relation to their clothing choices and consumption patterns in the mid-1950s and 1960s, but time constraints, so familiar to all scholars, but perhaps particularly so to those working in British institutions, made this impossible. Such work will have to wait for another time or another researcher.

5. On the Kinsey Report, as well as other forties and fifties scholarship on sexual practice and behavior, see Segal 1994: 87–9.
6. A close comparison of thirties and forties *Esquire* to early *Playboy* should yield some very interesting results and should illustrate that the latter was not as original as Hefner and his biographers would like the world to believe. Unfortunately, these issues of *Esquire* are not available in the UK.
7. Hefner did celebrate the writing and energy of the Beats in *Playboy*, however. See, for example, Herbert Gold *et al.*, "The Beat Mystique," *Playboy,* Vol. 5, No. 2 (February 1958): 20–6, 50, 74–5, 84–7 and Jack Kerouac, "The Origins of the Beat Generation," *Playboy,* Vol. 6, No. 6 (June 1959): 31–2, 42, 79.
8. Emphasis in the original.
9. For example, in May 1974 and August 1975 Robert L. Green presented two articles on "attire" entitled "Loose Threads" and "Loose Living." The fantasy at the core of these spreads was overtly heterosexual sex, rather than exotic foreign climes.
10. Such an argument seems to be an oversimplified version of one first published in the late 1970s by Angela McRobbie. She was exploring the construction of what she called "romantic individualism" in *Jackie,* a British teenage girls' magazine. In the article McRobbie actually wrote: "In fact, women's and girls' weeklies occupy a privileged position. Addressing themselves solely to a female market, their concern is with promoting feminine culture for their readers. They define and shape the woman's world, spanning every stage from childhood to old age . . . There are no male equivalents to these products. Male magazines tend to be based on particular leisure pursuits or hobbies, motorcycling, fishing, cars or even pornography . .. there are a variety of leisure options available, many of which involve participation outside the home" (McRobbie 1991: 83). Other early work on women's magazines made similar points. See, for example, White 1970 and Winship 1987.

Acknowledgments

I would like to thank the librarians at the New York Public Library for their assistance. The London College of Fashion's (LCF) Research Fund has made this work possible through a part-time Research Fellowship and a travel grant specifically for this project; I am extremely grateful and wish to particularly thank Elizabeth Rouse and Norma Starszakowna of LCF. For advice and support during the research and writing of this article, I wish to thank: the anonymous reader for this journal, Christopher Breward, Marjorie Bryer, Caroline Cox, Janene Furness, Jack Lechner, Sam Maser, and Adam Tooze, as well as the students on the History and Theory Pathway of the MA in Fashion Studies at LCF, who offered their comments on an earlier version of this piece.

References

Breward, Christopher. 1999. *The Hidden Consumer: Masculinities, Fashion and City Life 1860–1914*. Manchester and New York: Manchester University Press.

Chenoune, Farid. 1993. *A History of Men's Fashion*, trans. from the French by Deke Dusinbere. Paris: Flammarion.

Cohan, Steven. 1996. "So Functional for its Purposes: Rock Hudson's Bachelor Apartment in Pillow Talk." In Joel Sanders (ed), *Stud: Architectures of Masculinity*, pp. 28–41. Princeton, NJ: Princeton University Press. (This book also reprints the two original *Playboy* articles on the "Playboy Penthouse Apartment" on pp. 54–67.)

Craik, Jennifer. 1993. *The Face of Fashion: Cultural Studies of Fashion*. London and New York: Routledge.

Dines, Gail. 1995. "'I Buy It for the Articles': Playboy Magazine and the Sexualization of Consumption." In Gail Dines and Jean M. Humez (eds), *Gender, Race and Class in Media: A Text-Reader*, pp. 254–62. Thousand Oaks, CA, London and New Delhi: Sage Publications.

Dyer, Richard. 1997. *White*. London: Routledge.

Ehrenreich, Barbara. 1983. "Playboy Joins the Battle of the Sexes." In *The Hearts of Men: American Dreams and the Flight from Commitment*, pp. 42–51. New York: Anchor Press, Doubleday.

Fass, Paula S. 1977. *The Damned and the Beautiful: American Youth in the 1920s*. Oxford and New York: Oxford University Press.

Gold, Herbert *et al.* 1958. "The Beat Mystique." *Playboy*, Vol. 5, No. 2 (February 1958): 20–6, 50, 74–5, 84–7.

Green, Robert L. 1959a. "The Look of a Winner: Speed Week in Nassau Sets the Pace for Sports Car Fashions." *Playboy*, Vol. 6, No. 4 (April 1959): 28–30, 89.

——. 1959b. "Wardrobe for a Jet Weekend: The Continent is Just Seven Hours from Broadway." *Playboy*, Vol. 6, No. 5 (May 1959): 38–9.

——. 1960. "Meet Me at the Club: Right Raiment for Three Sporting Propositions." *Playboy*, Vol. 7, No. 4 (April 1960): 37–8, 101.

——. 1974. "Loose Threads." *Playboy*, Vol. 21, No. 5 (May 1974): 125–7.

——. 1975. "Loose Living." *Playboy*, Vol. 22, No. 8 (August 1975): 114–15.

Halberstam, David. 1993. *The Fifties*. New York: Fawcett Columbine.

Hefner, Hugh M. 1963. "The Playboy Philosophy. Part Two: *Playboy*'s editor-publisher spells out—for friends and critics alike—our guiding principles and editorial credo." *Playboy*, Vol. 10, No. 1 (January 1963): 41–52.

Kerouac, Jack. 1959. "The Origins of the Beat Generation." *Playboy*, Vol. 6, No. 6 (June 1959): 31–2, 42, 79.

Kessie, Jack J. 1955a. "The Well-Dressed Playboy: *Playboy*'s Position on Proper Male Attire." *Playboy*, Vol. 2, No. 2 (January 1955): 38–9.

——. 1955b. "Well-Groomed Featherweights for Spring: They're Light

on the Man and His Wallet." *Playboy,* Vol. 2, No. 5 (May 1955): 27.
——. 1955c. "The Basic Wardrobe." *Playboy,* Vol. 2, No. 9 (September 1955): 27–8, 34, 42.
——. 1955d. "Summa Cum Style." *Playboy,* Vol. 2, No. 10 (October 1955): 18–19, 52.
——. 1957. "The Marks of the Well-Dressed Man: A Top-to-Bottom Take-out on the Fine Points of Fashion." *Playboy,* Vol. 4, No. 3 (March 1957): 47, 69–70.
Kidwell, Claudia Brush and Valerie Steele (eds). 1989. *Men and Women: Dressing the Part.* Washington, DC: Smithsonian Institution Press.
McRobbie, Angela. 1991. *Feminism and Youth Culture: From* Jackie *to* Just Seventeen. Boston: Unwin Hyman.
May, Elaine Tyler. 1988. *Homeward Bound: American Families in the Cold War Era.* New York: Basic Books.
Miller, Russell. 1984. *Bunny: The Real Story of Playboy.* London: Michael Joseph.
Mort, Frank. 1996. *Cultures of Consumption: Masculinities and Social Space in Late Twentieth-Century Britain.* London: Routledge.
Nixon, Sean. 1996. *Hard Looks: Masculinities, Spectatorship and Contemporary Consumption.* London: University College London Press.
Paoletti, Jo Barraclough. 1985. "Ridicule and Role Models as Factors in American Men's Fashion Change, 1880–1910." *Costume,* No. 19 (1985): 121–34.
"Playboy's Penthouse Apartment." 1956a. *Playboy*, Vol. 3, No. 9 (September 1956): 54–60.
"Playboy's Penthouse Apartment, Part II ." 1956b. *Playboy*, Vol. 3, No. 10, (October 1956): 65–70.
Reed, Christopher. 1996. "Introduction." In *Not at Home: The Suppression of Domesticity in Modern Art and Architecture,* ed. Christopher Reed, pp. 7–17. London: Thames and Hudson.
Rutherford, Blake. 1957. "Ivy in Action: The Right Look for the Beach, Boating, Tennis and the Links." *Playboy,* Vol. 4, No. 7 (July 1957): 20–2.
——. 1958. "Formal Forecast: The Return to Black." *Playboy,* Vol. 5, No. 1 (January 1958): 60–2.
Segal, Lynne. 1994. *Straight Sex: The Politics of Pleasure.* London: Virago.
Votolato, Gregory. 1998. *American Design in the Twentieth Century.* Manchester and New York: Manchester University Press.
Walkerdine, Valerie. 1990. *Schoolgirl Fictions.* London and New York: Verso.
White, Cynthia L. 1970. *Women's Magazines 1693–1968.* London: Michael Joseph.
Wilson, Elizabeth. 1985. *Adorned in Dreams: Fashion and Modernity.* London: Virago.
Winship, Janice. 1987. *Inside Women's Magazines.* London: Pandora Press.

Fashion Theory, Volume 4, Issue 4, pp.467–486
Reprints available directly from the Publishers.
Photocopying permitted by licence only.

Language of the PurSuit: Cary Grant's Clothes in Alfred Hitchcock's "North by Northwest"

Ulrich Lehmann

Dr. Ulrich Lehmann is Senior Lecturer and Post-Doctoral Research Fellow at the Kent Institute of Art & Design in Rochester (GB). His book *Tigersprung: Fashion in Modernity* is published by The MIT Press in November 2000.

Introduction

When an English expert on the films of Alfred Hitchcock published a revised version of his study from the late 1960s, he bemoaned in his new introduction the fact that semiotic and structuralist views had pervaded film studies in an unqualified manner. In his criticism (Wood 1991: 8) he singled out the "constantly recurring, peculiarly irritating trait" of being told "[Roland] Barthes shows that . . .".

In the course of this essay I will be repeatedly claiming 'Roland Barthes shows that . . .'—or something to that effect. Not out of academic petulance or slavish adherence to a safe and established mode of interpretation, but because I regard the structuralist approach as the most appropriate when analyzing Hitchcock's *North by Northwest*. For me, this film has a visual cinematic narrative that offers much more surface than depth, more disguises than realities and more commodified images than meaning. I will argue that Hitchcock's film and the role that Cary Grant plays in it are explained best by looking at appearances—precisely because they are deceptive—and not at hermeneutical codes, cinematic quotations or self-referential truths.[1] Because the outermost surface of this film's narrative—I am discounting cinematic techniques—is occupied by the costumes, my argument will be exemplified by one of these, namely Grant's suit, which exerts a continuous presence throughout the duration of the film and thus stands analogous to the suit's normative presence in men's fashion throughout the nineteenth and twentieth centuries.

In attempting such a precise, some might say "restrictive," methodological focus I am aware that the essay can be criticized for not talking sufficiently about Hitchcock and the intricacies of his film-making, and, likewise, for not probing deeply enough into the aspects of consumption in male fashion and its sociological significance. However, the original structuralist interpretation of mass media and commodities—something in which Barthes excelled—was politicized to a great degree. Thus I feel that a Hollywood tale about a spying game at the height of the Cold War offers a convincing topic to which to apply such a concentrated critical "reading." Furthermore, the care that Hitchcock took in deciding upon the costumes for his films—for *North by Northwest* he spent days with his female lead Eva Marie Saint at Bergdorf Goodman in New York to select her outfits—renders clothing an integral part of the interpretative *mise-en-scène*. Therefore the reproach of not taking Hitchcock seriously by concentrating on a mere suit can be countered by arguing that the director deliberately cultivated surfaces in order to expose the perfunctoriness of his subject-matter—a fact that the elaborate *über*theoretical discourses around the "meaning" of Hitchcockian cinema choose to eschew because otherwise their work would lose the ripeness of its references.

To develop my argument, I have selected the dozen scenes in which the suit explicitly works as a signifier on screen or is topical for the dialog, thus carrying a significance that considerably exceeds its function within the storyline.

Methodology

The sartorial details observed in the following are not to be taken as metaphors for behavioral patterns, nor are they meant to be symbolic for the character's psyche. They should be read first as visual signifiers within a semiotic analysis.

When Roland Barthes first elaborated in 1957 on such an analysis, reversing the dominance of semiotics over linguistics in favor of, perhaps surprisingly, fashion-writing, he established a tripartite analogy between fashion and language.

In his essay "Histoire et sociologie du vêtement" Barthes paralleled the linguistic classification of language and the socially commodified significance of clothes. In linguistics the differentiation exists between *langage*, the language spoken within an anthropological framework; *langue*, spoken within a cultural grouping or society; and *parole*, the individual manner of speaking everybody uses for him- or herself. This classification finds its equivalent in the differences between *vêtement*, clothing in general; *costume*, as national or cultural sign of recognition; and *habillement*, individual sartorial expression (Barthes 1957: 435).[2] *Langue* is seen by Barthes (1967a: 28) as an institution, "a body abstracted by constraints," similar to the formalist attire of the suit that constrains the corporeal. Whereas *parole* is the part within the institution that is momentarily chosen by the individual and actualized for means of communication, both verbal and sartorial.

A decade later, with the publication of *Système de la Mode*, Barthes altered the above distinction and switched *vêtement* and *costume*. The latter was reduced to the most general of meanings, while *vêtement* now became an equivalent to the structuralist *langue* (Barthes 1967a: 28). Yet by substituting *vêtement* for *costume*, Barthes lost something important in his application of clothing to writing (in its historical and cultural context): the literal connotation of the male suit—*le costume* in French. Because *langue* is defined as a "structural institution," its equivalent has to be the homonym of the suit, as the one sartorial constituent in men's fashion since the early part of the nineteenth century.[3] This shift, which is critically accounted for in Barthes's publications in the decade after his original essay,[4] obfuscates this significance of the suit, which represents the norm in a patriarchal and commodified Western society. Thus it is more fitting for the present argument to remain with the first study—quite apart from the fact that "costume" is used in English to denote the clothes of an actor, which patently is not what Grant wears in Hitchcock's film, because he essentially plays himself and not a character.

Barthes explained in his essay of 1957 that a matter of personal dressing ("un fait d'habillement") constitutes first of all a deteriorated, i.e. non-normative, state of *costume*. Yet this state can be transformed into a secondary *costume*, when the deterioration functions as a collective sign, as a value: a minimal variation of the suit can become a matter of *costume* itself, the moment it is rendered a normative constituent of a certain group, a notion particularly expressive in dandyism (Barthes 1957: 437). More recent 'post'-structuralist writing has qualified assessments such as the above as rather formulistic. Yet for me Barthes's (and also Michel Butor's (1974)) texts on clothing remain convincing indeed—not least because of their formalism.

In the following I will argue how the suit as the sartorial surface functions as a signifier in an old-fashioned narrative that tells of the hero's trials and tribulations, and shows him being pursued, ridiculed and assaulted until he liberates himself from normative constraints to gain first freedom of action, and then love and respect as an individual. That such "liberation" is ultimately but a perfunctory gesture that remains embedded in the normative confines of cinematic and social language has to be expected from a US production of the 1950s and does not conflict with the present reading of the film.

Scene 1

(First day, late afternoon; the Oak Room, Plaza Hotel, New York City)

The film *North by Northwest* was scripted by Ernest Lehman, shot by Robert Burks and directed by Alfred Hitchcock for release in July 1959. It is on the surface, which is what concerns me here, an espionage thriller in the best tradition of Hollywood's Cold War paranoia. The comical or absurd elements and the casting of Cary Grant as a Madison Avenue executive mistaken for a government spy who is chased and attacked until he turns the tables on his foes, adds the element of light-hearted entertainment to a sometimes convoluted tale of pursuit, betrayal and double bluff.

In the opening part of the film—I will adhere to its chronology, although, for obvious reasons, not go through it scene by scene—we encounter Roger Thornhill (played by Cary Grant) meeting with business associates in a Manhattan bar. He is dressed in a lightweight, three-buttoned gray suit, a white shirt with French cuffs, a gray silk tie, light-gray socks and dark brown shoes. His three companions are attired in dark suits: the character Mr. Wade with white tie and pochette, Mr. Nelson with a dark tie, and fellow advertising man Mr. Weltner with a somber red tie. In this scene, where Grant is seen sitting comparatively still for the first time, the observer is offered a contrasted reading of Thornhill versus the other characters in the film, a reading that functions through the clothes and is maintained until the very last part of the story.[5] This contrast, pertaining as much to the fictional persona as it does to the actor Grant, of whom Hitchcock asked nothing more than variations on his habitual superficial charm and ironic superiority, is established by clothing Thornhill in a bespoke suit by Savile Row tailors Kilgour, French & Stanbury—an establishment frequented by Grant as well.[6] The supporting cast in this scene offers off-the-peg backgrounds, providing the common sartorial language (*costume*) of the 1950s, so paradigmatically embodied by Gregory Peck's *Man in the Gray Flannel Suit* in the eponymous film of 1956. Grant/Thornhill sits cross-legged and mannered, displaying the (for an American audience, European) sophistication of assorted socks and brown shoes, while the other characters remain stiffly reserved behind their desk. His is therefore a *parole*, a subtle but clearly expressed deviation from the norm, which prompts speculations about his social and individual behavior.[7] In the subsequent dialogue these speculations are fueled by Lehman and Hitchcock, in the customary ironic subversion of his heroes' roles, by employing an oedipal *spiel* of Grant fussing about getting a message to his mother—a device that ridicules the polished *parole/habillement* of the actor almost as much as it throws his character into the subsequent turbulence of the narrative.

Scene 2

(First day, early evening; library of country mansion)

Thornhill, fatefully having been mistaken for the government spy George Kaplan, is taken to villain Philip Vandamm (played by James Mason) who, in the apparent guise of Lester Townsend, eyes up his opponent for a first sparring.

> Vandamm: "Not what I expected; a little taller, a little more polished than the others."
> Thornhill [*with heavy irony*]: "Oh, I'm so glad you are pleased, Mr. Townsend!"

Here, the sartorial surface of the suit begins to assert its dominance over all other epistemological strands in the narrative. Both men mistake each other for somebody else, yet both make no apparent effort to look through the respective guise. On the contrary, they seem to take positive delight in assessing the other's outer appearance.

Vandamm is attired in a three-piece, neo-Edwardian dark suit, and is wearing a slate-gray tie. He is to be read as somebody who is well-tailored, yet exceedingly so: his sartorial signifier is too respectable, too elaborately stiff to be telling the truth about the man, in dialectical relation with the relaxed elegance of Thornhill's suit, who stands like an actor—which Grant never lets us forget he is, in more than just one sense, throughout the film—in front of a (stage) curtain, awaiting applause or condemnation, which is duly forthcoming from the villain.

Scene 2b

Vandamm's sidekick Leonard (played by Martin Landau) enters the room in a fitted navy suit with a blue tie, taking Thornhill's handsome surface for nothing more (but also nothing less) than it is, while protecting his own views behind an equally polished mask; his reserve will break only in the film's climactic last quarter.

Vandamm: "Ah, Leonard. Have you met our distinguished guest?"
Leonard: "He is a well-tailored one, isn't he?!"

Thornhill's misplaced internalization of oedipal laws, hinted at in the beginning, finds its projection in the physical approval of himself by a criminal, who is—by common critical consent—cast as a gay character.

In his series of interviews, French director François Truffaut (1983: 107) praised Hitchcock for his decision to render Vandamm such a debonair character of immaculate dress and manners, because it adds "the element of homosexual rivalry, with the male secretary [i.e. Leonard] clearly jealous of [the heroine Eve Kendall, played by] Eva Marie Saint."[8]

Yet the matter is far from being so well-cut. Fastidiousness in dress here signifies a narcissistic core, which supports the sartorial surface of all three men. Thornhill's elegance is first and foremost to be read as a designed corrective to a loss of moral values: he drinks too much, depends too strongly on his mother, already has two failed marriages behind him and steals other people's taxis. Those who merely glance at him, read Thornhill as a well turned-out surface that is hard to resist or criticize. Yet even the comparatively relaxed care about his appearance generates the perception of his being too groomed and handsome, too polished in all walks of life, and too aloof in the presence of women, especially. All of which puts his masculinity in question—a speculation that pursued Grant as a film-star throughout his career, and one that Hitchcock evidently enjoyed playing with.

In Vandamm's case, sartorial elegance is a guise for a more sinister subversion of core values in contemporary society. His suit, as well as the mansion to which Thornhill is taken and his assorted entourage, is a respectable front, masking espionage whose ultimate aim is to destroy the American way of life. Logically, his accent and clothes appear out of place, alien (English in this case) to the eyes and ears of the contemporary audience.

Leonard's suit signifies concealment, too. It is a front for "immoral" desires: the tailoring accommodates the gun that is later used for intimidation and murder; the somber and anonymous cloth is used to deflect attention from any effeminate behavior (shorthand for indulgence in gay sex); and the tight stiffness of the cut emphasizes the extreme economy, or even lack, of movement that betrays the single-minded pursuit of an unsocial ideal.

Scene 2c

In the ensuing struggle, Thornhill is forced on to the sofa and plied with Bourbon; the suit is seriously assaulted and soiled for the first time. Indeed, here one begins to read "the suit" exclusively as a signifier and the character as the signified: the hero is defined through his surface and the pursuit in the course of the film's narrative concentrates on the garment, whose light gray wool absurdly distinguishes the fugitive in his quest.

The fact that the cloth and shape of the suit show remarkable endurance and make a complete recovery from the pursuits and assaults in the preceding scenes, must be read as Hitchcock's effort to present the hero as a stable and identifiable commodity to the audience. Although his superficial *parole* might be suspicious, the actual signifiers, the suit as a sartorial constituent, the pristine white shirt and the straight tie, must remain intact. Nothing is torn, frayed or irreparably soiled. The hero always looks as if the general form of his garment, his *costume/langue*, that is the underlying adherence to the sartorial and social norm, cannot be penetrated; the American way of life (at least in perfunctory perception) cannot be seriously damaged or turned inside-out.

So Thornhill escapes by driving intoxicated with turned-up lapels and crumpled suit down a cliff road; he is picked up by the police and spends the rest of the night in jail. The next morning he is questioned, fined and subsequently released. Still wearing the same suit, he then attempts to peel away at least one of the surfaces in the narrative, that is, his mistaken identity as George Kaplan.

Scene 3

(Second day, around noon; room 796 at the Plaza Hotel, New York City)

Thornhill clandestinely enters Kaplan's room accompanied by his mother Clara Thornhill (played by Jessie Royce Landis). A valet delivers a black suit from the dry cleaner, affirming that his order came from the telephone and not from the owner of the suit himself.

> Thornhill: "I am beginning to think nobody in the hotel has actually seen Kaplan."
> Mother: "Maybe he has his suits mended by invisible weavers."

This statement appears enigmatic, even for the highly irrational character that the mother embodies (with the absence of a "father," any hope for a reality principle within this oedipal dependence seems to have been abandoned from the start). However, what Clara Thornhill actually hints at is an invisible power that mends and repairs the surface of the social fabric. In the case of the film's narrative, as we will learn later, this power is the government agency dealing in counter-espionage, who eventually assist Thornhill to regain his position in society. The construct of "George Kaplan"—whom we now suspect, along with Thornhill, of hardly being traceable—is only signified by a dark suit whose anonymous and ordinary sartorial language prevents any identification through a possible *parole*.

Scene 3b

Thornhill takes the cleaned suit from the wardrobe and slips on the jacket. Awkwardly tailored, it is too wide in the shoulders and waist, whereas the sleeves are much too short for Thornhill's arms. Uneasy about such an affront to his sartorial sensibilities, he shifts his shoulders and looks accusingly at his protruding left shirt sleeve and cuff.

Mother: "I don't think that one does anything for you."

Scene 3c

Thornhill takes the trousers and holds them in front of him. The waist is too wide, and the cut is conservative, with badly executed turn-ups when compared to the perfect length of his own trouser legs, which fall gracefully on to the polished surface of his shoes.

Mother [*ironically*]: "Ah now, that's much better."
Thornhill: "Obviously, they have mistaken me for a much shorter man."

Thornhill's/Grant's *parole* is not yet easily subsumed into the clothing mainstream of *langue*—much as his work as an advertising executive has schooled him in the past constantly to think of new words and sentences repeatedly to re-express the selfsame commodities—to find new surfaces for old products, so to speak.

The sartorial shell of Kaplan's suit is not distinguished enough for the hero; worse still, it is inadequately short. And one need not be aware of Hitchcock's penchant for amateur psychoanalysis and for popularizing Freudian ideas in his films (cf. *Marnie*, *Psycho*), to read the shortness of the sleeves and trousers as what it is meant to be: the inferiority of one male member in contrast to another.

The fact that the mother ironically praises the shortness of the trousers indicates how completely oedipal control has been exerted on the hero. Normative *langue* is preferred over individual *parole*. Even if the former is ill-fittingly short, it is sanctioned by societal and maternal judgment precisely because it is impotent, that is, less threatening or suspicious.[9]

Scene 4

(Second day, evening; sleeping compartment on the "Twentieth Century Ltd." train from New York to Chicago)

Having added the accusation of being a murderer to his already convoluted assortment of characters, Thornhill is now pursued on to the fast train from New York to Chicago, where he is taken in—in the most improbable of manners—by the industrial designer Eve Kendall (Eva Marie Saint), who hides Thornhill in the upper bunk of her compartment. After the immediate danger has passed, the hero is released from his confinement. When the bed is lowered, Thornhill removes a pair of broken sunglasses from the breast pocket of his suit, which—miraculously—appears immaculate despite the cramped conditions. The encounter with Eve might have broken one of the surfaces, the reflecting, concealing one of the sunglasses; but Thornhill's individual sartorial surface still remains untouched.

On the contrary, in embracing Eve, still fully clothed, Thornhill is reminded of what makes him attractive: the fact that he is a well-dressed commodity whose inner feeling or epistemic situation mean less to his surroundings than the sartorial signifier that clothes him.

Scene 5

Thornhill: "What else do you know?"
Eve: "You've got taste in clothes, taste in food . . ."
Thornhill: "And taste in women. I like your flavor."

In the profusion of his various roles, advertising executive, man-about-town, doting son, alleged government spy, suspected murderer and, now, sophisticated lover, the aspiration and danger within the cultural discourse of 1950s America are projected upon the surface of Thornhill/Grant. There appears to be no conflict between the made-to-measure clothes and the identity tailored to each situation of the pursuit.[10]

The three linguistic shifts that Barthes observed in the transposition of sartorial commodity to language are also manifest in the Thornhill character: the "real" shifts to "image"; the "real" shifts to "language," i.e. it is described; and, thirdly, the "image" itself shifts to "language." And the linguistic operation that functions in fashion writing applies in equal measure to the narrative around the hero in *North by Northwest*, multifaceted as he is.[11] Instead of Thornhill or Grant (it is difficult to distinguish an objective or disinterested "real" in the context of Hollywood) we get an immaculate attire, seemingly indestructible. This "image" is perpetually thematized in the film. It is chased, crumpled and squashed, but also constantly referred to and discussed within the "language" of the film, both in visual and dialog form.

When Thornhill leaves the train with Eve, he is (if only for a very brief period of time), yet in another guise which has been purchased from a porter. Walking beside her, Thornhill becomes concerned about his "image" or rather the real state of his suit.

Scene 6

(Third day, nine o'clock in the morning; platform at Central Station, Chicago)

Thornhill: "Which one of these has my suit in it?"
Eve: "The small one, underneath your right arm."
Thornhill: "Oh thanks. That ought to do the suit a lot of good."
Eve: "I am sure Mr. Kaplan won't mind a few wrinkles."

The "image" shifts to "language" as the perfected surface of the clothing becomes a cause for concern. Never mind the real danger of the situation Thornhill finds himself in, pursued by spies, by detectives and policemen on the concourse, and by Eve, who, unbeknownst to him conspires with Vandamm and Leonard: his concern is the creases in his suit where there ought to be none.

But one has to sympathize with Thornhill; apart from the suit there is nothing left for him. His bourgeois identity has been stripped away during the narrative and his identification, which has been supported so powerfully by his elegance and sense of style, is now entirely dependent on the continuity of his apparel.

Eve's response to this ontological dilemma appears casual. Why indeed should George Kaplan mind creases in the suit?! For her part she can be sure that the meeting between Kaplan and Thornhill will never take place, while the latter should deduce from Kaplan's badly tailored suit (not to mention his dandruff) that it is not the state of his appearance that matters, but the fact that it is not detected in the first place.

Yet again, Thornhill changes back into the stylistic motif of the gray cloth, which looks as cleaned and pressed as in the first scene, the ironed white shirt and the immaculate tie. As vaguely defined as his character may remain, his pursuers should by now pay particular attention to the sartorial shell as the only means of identification; yet precisely this signifier is still worn by Thornhill for his promised meeting with Kaplan on the plains of rural Illinois.

Scene 7

(Third day, early afternoon; Prairie Stop, Highway 41, Illinois)

Thornhill stands alienated in his city suit in an empty and open landscape, waiting in the wind and dust of passing vehicles for his rendezvous with Kaplan. He goes through a well-choreographed sequence of moves, signaling his anticipation. Hands are thrust into trouser pockets only to be taken out again, cuffs are tugged, and the jacket is adjusted and finally unbuttoned.

Just in time—as a biplane ("dusting crops where there ain't no crops") begins to swoop down and fire on him. Thanks to some impressive sprints, some headlong dives into the field and a clever escape trick under a truck, which is then hit by the plane, Thornhill manages to survive this, the most brutal assault on his character so far. The absurd magnitude of this pursuit—why resort to the elaborate plan of chasing a man over an open field in a plane, when you could as easily lure him into a hotel room in Chicago to finish him off?!—seems to complete the hero's degradation. His elegant *parole* is subjected to murderous (though cinematically dramatized) reality, and for the first time in the film's narrative an existentialist void is created around, if not within, the character.

Eventually, Thornhill returns to Chicago to seek out Kaplan. In the hotel he becomes aware of Eve's betrayal.

Scene 8

(Third day, evening; room 463 in the Ambassador Hotel, Chicago)

Although he is covered in flecks and patches of white and sand-colored dust, which are disapprovingly noticed by the concierge, in substance Thornhill's appearance is miraculously unaffected. Again, the beholder notices no tears or rents in the cloth; the crease in the trousers is sharp, the lie of the collar immaculate, the shirt remains stubbornly ironed and the tie perfectly in place. Again, the effects of existential danger are merely touching the surface; the essence of the suit, as the signifier, stays intact. However, for the first time a sense of inner conflict or drama appears; not enough actually to affect the sign of Thornhill/Grant, but clearly manifest in the visual communication with Eve's character:

> Eve: ". . . I want you to leave right now . . . So, please: Good-bye, good luck. No conversations; just leave."
> Thornhill: "Right away?"
> Eve: "Yes."
> Thornhill: "No questions asked?!"
> Eve: "Yes."
> Thornhill: "No, I can't do that."
> Eve: "Please!"
> Thornhill: "After dinner."
> Eve: "Now!"
> Thornhill: "After dinner; fair is fair."
> Eve: "All right. On one condition: that you let the hotel valet do something with this suit first. You belong in the stockyards, looking like that."

What appears as a commonplace metaphor of bourgeois cleanliness, might suggest that a soiled Thornhill is not a Thornhill to speak of. His identity so much depends on the clothing-"image" that any imperfection can shift it back to the "real."

Scene 8b

Thornhill sits on the bed, assuming the same confident position as in the hotel bar at the beginning of the film. He telephones the valet while trying to decipher Eve's note-pad to find out her true identity and intentions:

> Thornhill: "How quickly can you get a suit sponged and pressed?—Yes, fast."
> - . . . -
> Thornhill: "Twenty minutes!?—Fine . . ."
> - . . . -
> Thornhill [*to Eve who is in the bathroom*]: "He'll be right up."
> Eve: "Better take your things off."

Thornhill empties his pockets—still not devoid of a small amount of banknotes and some personal belongings.

Scene 8c

> Thornhill [*walks up to Eve from behind*]: "Yeah. Now, what can a man do with his clothes off for twenty minutes?—Could he not have taken an hour?!"
> Eve [*slipping off his jacket*]: "You could always take a cold shower."
> Thornhill: "That's right.—When I was a little boy, I wouldn't even let my mother undress me."
> Eve: "You are a big boy now."
> Thornhill [*in shirtsleeves*]: "Yes."

Such an exchange is very much part of Hitchcock's cinematic vocabulary. In order to alter the tempo or ease the tension within a thriller, elements of "ironic" dialog are woven into the narrative. In this and other cases, the director (and scriptwriter) seem to enjoy overt references to Freud, who had pervaded American cultural consciousness in the 1950s through the dissemination of psychoanalytical practice. Obviously, the sexual overture and subsequent frustration, followed by a transposition of oedipal dependence, is introduced to suggest the singularity of Eve's position towards Thornhill. The fact, however, that she is allowed actively to remove part of the suit suggests an interest in her peeling away the surface and getting at Thornhill's identity. Ironically, this occurs at the very moment when he himself decides to accept the double guise of an alleged agent.

After having accused Eve of teasing and criminal role-play, Thornhill walks into the bathroom and relinquishes the last part of his suit to her.

Scene 8d

Eve: "Trousers please."
Thornhill: "Certainly.—Here you are."

In handing the suit to the valet, Eve inadvertently assists Thornhill in a sartorial rite of passage into the spying game. Like the fictitious George Kaplan, for whom Eve, Vandamm and Leonard still mistake Thornhill, he himself has his suit now cleaned in a hotel, by invisible hands and, one suspects, with the cleaning bill picked up by some imaginary source.

Without his suit, yet still in his shirt and tie (Freud and his disciple Stefan Hollós would surely have commented on such a display),[12] Thornhill then performs his first act as a spy proper by deciphering Eve's note.

Scene 9

(Third day, night; auction room of [. . .] & Oppenheim Galleries on 1212 North Michigan Ave, Chicago)

Thornhill, freshly showered and in his sponged and pressed suit, his shoes polished, enters the auction room to approach Vandamm, standing with Eve and Leonard at the front of the bidding public. Vandamm has now, despite the late hour, changed into a light gray suit with a dark tie; an unexpected sartorial *faux pas* by the fastidious spy. One assumes that Thornhill, who obviously has to continue wearing the same suit, would have known when to change into dark evening attire.

The contrast in tailoring—Thornhill's fitted suit which depends on the perfect cut of the shoulders and the collar, versus Vandamm's suit with its slightly over-cut shoulders and wider sleeves—signifies the conflict of *parole* and *langue*. Gray does not equal gray; Thornhill's cloth is identifiably individual, while Vandamm intends to submit to the general sartorial language that is apparent in the gray-suited men around him (one of them being "The Professor," who supervises the spying game).

Leonard wears his habitually stiff, dark suit and blue tie, which is tight at the waist and slim in the shoulders, tentatively suggesting the cut of a feminine *tailleur*—beneath which he is sporting his gun.

In a genuine flashback to the "screwball" school of comedy, Thornhill upsets the proceedings in order to get arrested by the police. In the ensuing punch-up his suit is ruffled once more, his sleeves again manhandled by police officers.

Scene 10

(Third day, night; Chicago airport)

"The Professor" (played by Leo G. Carroll) and Thornhill finally get to meet and talk about the past days. He is confronted with an elaborate spy story of bluff and counter-bluff, as well as with the fact that, despite the sartorial *langue* discussed in the New York hotel room, there is no such person as George Kaplan:

> Thornhill: "What do you mean, 'there is no such person'?! I've been in his hotel room, I tried on his clothes. He has got short sleeves and dandruff."
> The Professor: "Believe me Mr. Thornhill, he doesn't exist.—Which is why I am going to have to ask you to go on being him for the next twenty-four hours."[13]

This controlling instantiation of the government agency appears to accept now Thornhill's *parole*, which, although deviating from the social construct they are meant to uphold, has become a form of *langue*: a value, a sign for the collective, with whom he begins to be identified more and more. By taking him into the societal fold of gray suited men who are productive for the common good and directed towards normative material goals (which the urbane and cynical advertising executive was not necessarily), Thornhill's suit loses importance as *parole* and begins to relinquish its leading role in the narrative.

Scene 11

(Fourth Day, morning; self-service restaurant opposite Mount Rushmore, Rapid City, South Dakota)

Thornhill meets with Vandamm, who is absurdly dapper in a "landed gentry" sort of way, in his light tweed suit and green waistcoat with matching tie and dark hat. He proposes a trade-off between Eve and a safe passage for the spies. Eve then provokes a public conflict that climaxes in her putting two bullet holes into Thornhill's suit before fleeing screaming from the scene. Leonard, ever suspicious of the surfaces presented to him, is confronted with a layer of fake blood on the Professor's hand. Finally, Thornhill's body is carried away—covered by a matching gray blanket—to a clearing in a wood, where he meets Eve.

Despite this last and most intimate assault, the shooting from close range, the suit is as immaculate as ever. Undamaged, it signifies once again the deceptive surface of the narrative; and the beholder understands that the blank bullets were just another "reality" that has turned out to be a fictional construct.

In order to prevent Thornhill from joining Eve in her final role-play, the Professor instructs a state trooper to punch Thornhill out. The scene where he hits the pine needles is the last instance where we see the suit.

Scene 12

(Fourth day, afternoon; room in hospital)

We look at Thornhill without his clothes for the first time, pacing restlessly in a towel before a radio. The Professor unlocks the door to the hospital room.

> The Professor: "Here we are."
> Thornhill: "Hello." The Professor [*throwing a box on the bed where Thornhill rests*]: "Slacks and a shirt . . ." [*waving a shoe box*]—"And these . . .".
> Thornhill: "Thank you."
> The Professor: "That'll do for you around here, for the next couple of days."

From this moment on, and ironically in his confinement, Thornhill is initiated officially into the spying game. A few hours ago he had, for the first time, played a part that was not for himself, made to impress or deceive other members of his social set; this time his role play was designed to assist society at large. He has been drafted into the ranks of the government. Logically, this needs to be ritualized by a change of clothing.

Thus the Professor, as the representative of normative society, has bought for him sartorial signifiers that are perfect examples of the popular American *costume/langue*: a wide, button-down, "Brooks Brothers" type of shirt, slate-gray pleated trousers, a black leather belt and black penny loafers.

Yet the outfit is not "respectable" in terms of bourgeois apparel; it is absurdly casual. The Professor qualifies his choice with the line: "That'll do for you *around here*"—meaning the hospital room to which he has to confine himself in order not to expose Eve as a fraud. Nevertheless, this outfit provides Thornhill with the security of a socially sanctioned *costume/langue*—although in the guise of leisurewear—that he requires to step out of his previous egotistical character (with its signifier, the polished *parole/habillement* of the gray suit) and, after his escape act, to become active in saving "his girl," the American way of life and Western civilization as a whole.

Despite such inherent "logic," there are also cinematic reasons for a switch in Thornhill's clothing: Hitchcock himself said that he required a large white shirt to distinguish Grant from the other actors during the long shots and tracking movements in the dark on Mount Rushmore.

Indeed, given Thornhill's/Grant's acrobatics in the last part of the film it makes more sense to dress him in casual wear than in a suit, although the latter had not prevented his character from performing stunts and engaging in fights beforehand.

Conclusion

It would be simplistic to read the eventual change of attire from conservative mainstay to casualwear, from timeless Savile Row to fifties Americana, or from individualized bespoke suit to mass-produced clothing, as a sartorial *éducation sentimentale* that heralds a change of attitude in the hero. Granted, the narrative suggests that Thornhill learns to assume responsibility in the end, that he recognizes the need for commitment towards relationships, and perhaps even to society at large, and that he appears determined to fulfill his role as an altruistic and engaged citizen from then on.

But is this not again another surface? Is there anything in his vague characterization to show us a glimpse of Thornhill's true identity?

As a commercial enterprise a Hollywood film has to end on a moral high note, and Hitchcock abided by such narrative norms. However, the emphasis that has been placed throughout the greatest part of the film on the suit, the *parole*, which appears deliberately, even cynically, superficial, suggests that the interest in the surface is much greater than any attempt to account for the character's internal development or his psychological progress.

Barthes's reading of fashion can be extended to the appearance of Thornhill/Grant in Hitchcock's film because commodified products surround and clothe the character. One of these products develops in a manner analogous to that of a linguistic constituent in (visual) language; not for any metaphorical or symbolic reason—after all it is just a contemporary suit—but as an integral part of the narrative, as a visual lead that constructs thematic coherence.

As such the hunt for the spy appears on the surface as merely a narrative that envelops a central sartorial motif, and the story of the film is therefore indeed written in the language of a pure suit.

Notes

1. See Hartman (1981: 14) for a description of Alain Resnais's *L'Année dernière à Marienbad*: "The face of those worded images remains smooth, slippery; they are pictures determined not to be words; they insist on a pictographic as well as semiotic content, a nonsensous visual stenography." While this is a commonly held view of such deliberate artificiality—common because American critics tend to regard thus

European "art-house" cinema that eschews clear narratives—it can be applied in equal measure to Hitchcock's rather more superficial products of the 1950s and 1960s.

The different views on Hitchcock's cinematic narrative are extended to a general reflection between the stylistic and the structural as "dialectically related projections of the two poles of the dilemma of modernist form" by Fredric Jameson (1992: 48).

An account of *North by Northwest* that employs Barthes's structuralist reading of texts can be found in Bellour 1975; an extended version of the essay is contained in Bellour 1979: 131–246. After the initial application of structuralism the texts turn to a Lacanian analysis and, in the later version, to a minute reading of the sequence on the Illinois plains.

2. See also Ferdinand de Saussure's disciple Charles Bally who in 1909 already had considered "fashion itself a form of language [*langage*]" (Bally 1970 [1909]: 11–12).
3. See e.g. Harvey 1995: 23–39 and Breward 1999: 24–53.
4. One reason for this shift can be traced back to an earlier essay on "Les Maladies du costume de théâtre" that Barthes republished in conjunction with "L'Activité structuraliste" as an important early example of his methodological approach. In this essay the term *costume* was exclusively employed to denote clothes worn on stage or in films. Therefore it seems as if the shift in meaning from *costume* to *vêtement* became necessary because the latter had no overtones of masquerade or garb (Barthes 1964 [1955]: 53–62, 1964 [1963]: 213–20).

   Introducing Barthes to the Anglo-American reader, the *Partisan Review* published these two essays together: see "The Structuralist Activity" and "The Diseases of the Costume" (Barthes 1967b: 82–97).
5. See Naremore 1988: 214–17 for an enthusiastic celebration of Grant's dress sense in *North by Northwest*.
6. William Rothman (1983: 13) wrote: "But a further joke is in the idea that Cary Grant could ever be mistaken for a 'Roger Thornhill' in the first place. Roger Thornhill is only a fictional character, created by Hitchcock and subject to his authorship—no more real than the non-existent decoy 'George Kaplan'. Hitchcock's real agent is—Cary Grant. Grant's complete visibility in the world of *North by Northwest* is an acknowledgment of his familiar way of inhabiting the screen."
7. Stanley Cavell (1981: 766) in his equation of *North by Northwest* with the theme of *Hamlet* locates a similar observation in the auction room-comedy halfway through the film. The demand on Thornhill is to ". . . be decorous, be socialized; but society has been forcing an identity and a guilt upon him that he does not recognize as his own, so the natural hope for a way out is to abdicate from that society."
8. See Corber 1993: 253n12; and "The Murderous Gays: Hitchcock's Homophobia" (Wood 1991: 336–57, 365).

Lesley Brill (1988: 9) sartorially connects the villains: "With their dark suits and cold refinement, VanDamm [*sic*] and Leonard are strongly linked when they first appear in Townsend's library."

9. See Bellour's "psychoanalytical" reading of the suit in this hotel room scene and the later one of Thornhill and Eve in Chicago—perhaps springing the "trap" that Lehman and Hitchcock laid out in view of such a suggested interpretation (1975: 255).
10. Again, cf. Hartman (1981: 23): "That film is almost too healthy. Roger learns vigilance without being traumatized. The psyche is not involved, or not as a perverse emptiness, always escaping from being watched and therefore ever wary."
11. A less structuralist reading of the "image" comes from Jameson (1992: 48): "The main body of the film can then be seen as a quest or a test, trial by fire, struggle with the adversary, the experience of betrayal, action not with images but within images . . .".
12. See Freud 1940 [1900]: 357–8; Hollós 1923: 73 and Flügel 1930: 27.
13. A dialectical pun by the scriptwriter; "determinatio est negatio," Spinoza would have said. There exists no Kaplan, yet his existence has to be continuous.

References

Bally, Charles. 1970 [1909]. *Traité de stylistique française, Vol.1*. Geneva: Georg.

Barthes, Roland. 1957. "Histoire et sociologie du vêtement." *Annales: Economies, Sociétés, Civilisations*, vol.12, no.3, June/September 1957: 430–41. Paris: Colin.

——. 1964 [1955]. "Les Maladies du costume de théâtre." In *Essais critiques*, pp. 53–62. Paris: Seuil. (Originally published in *Théâtre populaire* (Paris), no.12, March/April 1955.)

——. 1964 [1963]. "L'Activité structuraliste." In *Essais critiques*, pp. 213–20. Paris: Seuil. (Originally published in *Lettres nouvelles*, Paris, 1963.)

——. 1967a. *Système de la mode*. Paris: Seuil.

——. 1967b. "The Structuralist Activity" and "The Diseases of Costume," trans. R. Howard. *Partisan Review* (New York), vol.34, no.1 (Winter 1967): 82–8, 89–97.

Bellour, Raymond. 1975. "Le Blocage symbolique." Communications, no.23 ("Psychanalyse et cinéma"): 235–63. Paris: Seuil.

——. 1979. *L'Analyse du film*. Paris: Albatros.

Breward, Christopher. 1999. *The Hidden Consumer: Masculinity, Fashion and City Life 1860–1914*. Manchester: Manchester University Press.

Brill, Leslie. 1988. "*North by Northwest* and Romance." In *The Hitchcock Romance: Love and Irony in Hitchcock's Films*, pp. 3–21. Princeton, NJ: Princeton University Press.

Butor, Michel. 1974. "Mode et moderne." In *Répertoire IV*, pp. 399–414. Paris: Minuit.

Cavell, Stanley. 1981. "North by Northwest". *Critical Inquiry*, vol.7 (Summer 1981): 761–76. Chicago: University of Chicago Press.

Corber, Robert J. 1993. *In the Name of National Security: Hitchcock, Homophobia, and the Political Construction of Gender in Postwar America*. Durham, NC and London: Duke University Press.

Flügel, Joh[an]n Carl. 1930. *The Psychology of Clothes*. London: Hogarth.

Freud, Sigmund. 1940 [1900]. *The Interpretation of Dreams*, trans. J. Strachey. London: Hogarth.

Hartman, Geoffrey H. 1981. "Plenty of Nothing: Hitchcock's *North by Northwest*." *The Yale Review*, vol.71, no.1 (Autumn 1981): 13–27. New Haven, CT: Yale University Press.

Harvey, John. 1995. *Men in Black*. London: Reaktion.

Hollós, Stephan. 1923. "Schlangen und Krawattensymbolik." *Internationale Zeitschrift für Psychoanalyse*, vol.9: 73–4. Vienna and Zurich: Internationaler Psychoanalytischer Verlag.

Jameson, Fredric. 1992. "Spatial Systems in *North by Northwest*." In Slavoj Zizek (ed.), *Everything You Always Wanted to Know About Lacan (But Were Afraid To Ask Hitchcock)*, pp. 47–72. London: Verso.

Naremore, James. 1988. "Cary Grant in *North by Northwest* (1959)." In *Acting in the Cinema*, pp. 213–35. Berkeley, CA and London: University of California Press.

Rothman, William. 1983. "*North by Northwest*: Hitchcock's Monument to the Hitchcock Film." *North Dakota Quarterly*, vol.51 (Summer 1983): 11–23. Grand Forks, ND: University of North Dakota.

Truffaut, François. 1983. *Hitchcock: The Definitive Study of Alfred Hitchcock by François Truffaut*. New York: Simon & Schuster.

Wood, Robin. 1991. *Hitchcock's Films Revisited*. London: Faber & Faber.

Fashion Theory, Volume 4, Issue 4, pp.487–506
Reprints available directly from the Publishers.
Photocopying permitted by licence only.

John Stephen: A Carnaby Street Presentation of Masculinity 1957–1975

Alistair O'Neill

Alistair O'Neill is a lecturer and research fellow at the London College of Fashion. He is also the curator of Sho Gallery, London. Forthcoming work includes an exhibition titled "Between '68 and '76: Fashion Retailing in London."

It is recognized that, in the post-war period, British men began to participate more in the experience of shopping. With the aid of the advertising, marketing and retailing industries, masculine consumption not only increased, but was subject to the creation of new practices of shopping. In the case of buying clothes, these new practices were often moulded by entrepreneurs keen to fashion the development of a distinctive masculine style position. In turn, this created a situation where style positions were understood by consumption: by the space, place and location of the sale.

This article is concerned with the relationship between Carnaby Street, a London street transformed into a shopping destination of landmark status, and John Stephen, the entrepreneur credited with changing not only the street but also the notion of menswear. Drawing upon the recently acquired John Stephen archive at the Archive of Art and Design (Victoria and Albert Museum), the aim is to clarify the distinctions between retailer, consumer and retail area, extrapolating them from a moment of social history that remains heavily mythologized. It proposes that shops and shopping areas can be held responsible for the creation of new masculine style positions and that these identities are strongly bound to a popular understanding of these spaces, even to the point of disadvantage.

A Contemporary View

In a recent London exhibition staged in an unoccupied retail space by the architectural group FAT (Fashion, Architecture, Taste), the artists Tim Noble and Sue Webster designed a carrier bag for the clothing shop All Saints, just off Carnaby Street, that bore a Union Jack flag emblazoned with the slogan "British Rubbish." This wry design formed part of "Shopping," a project-cum-exhibition that commissioned carrier bag designs by over thirty artists and designers that were given away free with purchases from participating shops in the Carnaby Street area.

Although primarily intended to interweave the distinctly separate styles of consumption involved in shopping for art and shopping for clothes, the premise of the exhibition served as a paradigm laden with historical resonances for both a consideration of London's fashion history and the development of a distinctive masculine style position.

Particular bags made particular points. Thus the pop artist Peter Blake's brightly colored carrier that spelt "Go Shopping" in assorted burlesque Victorian capitals became emblematic of the appropriation of forms from popular memory *circa* 1966, with particular reference to the artist's design for the Beatles' Sergeant Pepper album cover and the ensuing fashion for military uniforms sold on Carnaby Street. In clear opposition to Blake's nostalgia, Noble & Webster's design paid obvious call to Carnaby Street's succeeding reputation as a cheap market for tourist goods, but also slated attempts at rebranded identity, even calling to mind the failed "I'm Backing Britain" economic campaign of 1968. As an article in *The Guardian* at the time of the campaign noted, "one stallholder said that most of the British rubbish is made abroad, although thought up here. They would like to sell British, but our manufacturers will not bustle up deliveries for the quick turnover Carnaby Street has—there is much speedier delivery by ordering goods through importing wholesalers. Ironically, some of it is re-exported" (*The Guardian*: 25/06/1968).

In the accompanying catalog essay written by Richard Benson, a former group editor of *The Face* and *Arena* magazines, the history of Carnaby Street as a shopping area is centered around a purchase of a black cape made by the author as a teenager. As a provincial youth in the early 1980s,

Benson's idea of Carnaby Street was largely informed by advertisements in the back of music magazines, which illustrated the accoutrements of subcultural dress in harsh line drawings. This was a technique used by many retailers on the street, who invested heavily in mail order to augment their takings.

For Benson, the act of consumption served as a means of accessing that element of metropolitan identity that he felt to be commensurate with his status as an emerging male teenager. Although by the 1980s Carnaby Street had become a clichéd rendition of its more discerning conception in the early 1960s, Benson claimed that it still held the same purpose for the emancipation of youth. Borrowing heavily from Nik Cohn's "overlooked" account of British menswear in the post-war period, "Today there are no Gentlemen," Benson laid the legacy of the road at the feet of John Stephen, the retailer once known as "King of Carnaby Street." A distinct lineage could be drawn from Stephen's opening his first boutique in 1957 to the motley array of shops participating in "Shopping" in and around Carnaby Street. The potential of such a genealogy to mirror a broader history of masculine consumption merits further attention.

John Stephen has been credited with the title "King of Carnaby Street" for his swift commercial assault on dressing the modern male youth of London in the 1960s. He was largely responsible for transforming a low-rent street of tobacconists into the central site for the consumption of "Swinging London." What is particular to this reputation is the accelerated density of Stephen's expansion. His business evolved from a single shop in 1957 to twenty-two in Greater London (nine of these with Carnaby Street addresses) by 1966. By 1975, the year that The John Stephen of London Group was wound up, the company had significantly expanded, employing four hundred staff, with two factories, a design team, a publicity department and thirty shops in Europe and the USA.

In British youth subcultural history he has earned a special place for offering an accelerated range of choice to young men eager for difference, and for constructing spaces conducive to both shopping and social interaction. Pictorial evidence confirms how the self-awareness of this consumption went beyond the confines of the shop fittings and was played out in a burgeoning street culture ripe for media attention. Within a history of post-war British men's dress, John Stephen appears as a symbol of "modernist" aspirations in appearances formulated into mod uniform for sale. Although not the first to understand the post-war potential for "drag" or casual separates, Stephen took Bill Green's example (Green was the owner of Vince's Man's Shop, where he had formerly worked as a salesman), applying a greater degree of business acumen so that Vince's largely homoerotic style was filtered for mass consumption. However, post-1965 the business was obscured by the rise of Chelsea bohemianism and the increasing commercial gluttony of Carnaby Street, which dulled its edge. Little is recorded about John Stephen beyond this point, a recent exception being a suit from 1970 given by the milliner David Shilling to

Figure 1
Tim Noble & Sue Webster, carrier bag design, "British Rubbish," produced for All Saints Ltd as part of the exhibition Shopping, organized by FAT, Carnaby Street, London, 1999. Reproduced with the kind permission of the artists.

the Victoria and Albert Museum and later reproduced in the catalog to the V&A exhibition "The Cutting Edge" on the history of British couture, where it is described as "looking curiously androgynous." While "authentic" beginnings are always of greater historical interest than commercial excess, greater clarification needs to be given to the obscuration accorded Stephen.

A Member of the Meritocracy

The supposed demise of John Stephen has a particular contemporary relevance given the recent airing of his portrait for the David Bailey Retrospective *Birth of the Cool* at the Barbican Gallery, London (and its reproduction in *David Bailey: Archive One*, published by Thames & Hudson). In its lack of historical clarity, the exhibition was a timely reminder of how a mythologizing tendency still prevails in the presentation of pictorial evidence from the 1960s. Central to this tendency is the need to account in some way for *Swinging London* as a concept, usually credited to *Time* magazine in 1966 but actually first discussed by the American John Crosby writing in *The Daily Telegraph* color supplement a year earlier (*The Daily Telegraph* 30/04/1965).

Jonathan Green's recently published history of the sixties counter-culture *All Dressed Up* places particular emphasis on the whimsical tone of the article and the flippancy of the journalist who claimed, among many other things, that London girls take to sex "as if it's candy." What is interesting is how these casual statements helped to define not only Swinging London but also the style in which it was reported. Green's comments on Crosby's interpretation of fashion retailers and designers are particularly apt:

> Mary Quant "and a bunch of other pretty Chelsea Birds" have revolutionized fashion; Julie Christie gets her name check, as do Bailey and "Terry" Donovan and Carnaby Street retailer John Stephen, obligatory poles on the make, although when it comes to fashion Crosby is soon out of Carnaby Street and even the King's Road, and heading back to the classier world of Blades, where Rupert Lycett-Green, the very model of a youthful upper-class dandy, set up to dress his peers. (Green 1998: 70)

Crosby is described as a kind of whirling *flâneur*, crossing class distinctions and metropolitan zones in a style wholly derived from the English aristocracy's knack for "mixing it" at social occasions. The term refers to the inclusion of artistic, bohemian and creative individuals, who existed outside upper-class society, but who were invited to social events to add what was then considered excitement and local color. The idea of "mixing it" was a strong catalyst to American onlookers, as Andrea Adam, a journalist at *Time* magazine, confirmed when recounting the "Swinging London" edition of 1966: "We perceived a classlessness coming from the aristocracy, who were very heavily involved too, that we found very attractive. People seemed easy-going about their titles" (Green 1998: 86). The *laissez-faire* attitude was also to be reflected in the reporting, where specificity and detail were often bleached by the reconfigured, journalistic narrative (lacing the term "mixing it" with a very different connotation). It is worth noting here that it was the very different "take" on the city that these articles made that helped Britons see London afresh, such was the allure of the American aesthetic.

This is further ramified by Christopher Booker's observation in his critique of British society in the period that in 1958 the upper-class and working-class young were meeting "in the new 'classless' middle ground of jeans and modern jazz, of 'hip' and 'cool', of casual Americanized clothes and casual Americanized speech that foreshadowed the pop culture to come" (Booker 1969: 133). This is of crucial importance to the formulation of the "New Establishment" as defined by the work of David Bailey, not only in foregrounding the origins of terms such as "cool," but also in setting a notion of "mixing it" within the consumption of clothing and style.

It is generally accepted by historians such as Green that Bailey's two publications of the 1960s are testaments to those who constituted this scene. His role in deciding who "was" and who "wasn't" in, largely defines those remembered for posterity. The first, *Bailey's Box of Pin-Ups* (1965) gave conceptual meaning to the newly found "in crowd." Inside a box lay assorted captioned pictures of individuals aiming to capture "the ephemeral glamour" of the transitory scene. This was then laid to rest with *Goodbye, Amen to All That: A Saraband for the Sixties* (1969), a book of many more portraits with a text by Peter Evans.

Booker identified the three main values that Bailey's portraiture gave to the foundation of the "New Establishment": "It was an image of 'youth,' 'vitality,' 'creativity,' 'originality.' 'life' and 'excitement.' Second, it was an image of classlessness . . . the third ingredient in the collective image was that it was 'revolt' against 'stuffy,' 'old-fashioned,' 'bourgeois convention'" (Booker 1969: 23).

This combination was regularly mixed and applied by the new media titles such as *Queen*, *Man About Town* and *The Sunday Times Magazine*, moving beyond the mere reporting of the said individuals towards a worded formula that could equate with a shift in society. It is the very closeness of this formula to the photographic style developed by Bailey that inverts it back to something mediatized, something that barely existed. (This is upheld by publications such as *David Bailey: Archive One*, which reproduces images used in magazine spreads as isolated photographs rather than as components of a designed visual statement of image and text.) It makes the stark black and whites seem like notoriety in the papers; the pores of the skin a stark reality, the flat backdrop color framing the portraits as unreal and "flat as a magazine page." This in turn served to gloss the specificity of the individual, so that "none of them [were] being described actually as a living individual in himself, but only representative as a kind of collective "image,' the different ingredients of which could be applied to any one of them interchangeably."

John Stephen was easily allied to the three prerequisites. The clipped story following his portrait in *Goodbye, Amen to All That* tells of the boy who worked in the menswear department of the Glasgow Co-op, who moved to London and worked double shifts to raise the money to open his first store, which became "the boom that made the most famous fashion carnival in the world: Carnaby Street." Accelerated transformation is the central motif of the definition, and it became synonymous with the designer. As a BBCTV interview of the same year underlined, "John, your success story follows classic lines of a boy who came to London and made good. How large is your group of companies now?" (BBC1TV, "A Quick Look Round": 9/2/1965). The combination of the young male on the periphery and metropolitan success was central to John Stephen's appeal and to the consumption of his clothes by suburban boys. What is interesting is how this definition marked Stephen's reputation; how the looseness in the construction of the prerequisites and their application were eventually to mark him as fixed and essentially different from others in the field of menswear.

In examining the portrait by Bailey, Stephen's face almost completely obscured by an emanating curl of cigar smoke save a piercing eye to camera, the viewer is reminded of the conventions of Hollywood portrait photography. Yet the soft, desirous focus of old is exchanged for hard-edged contrasts (unparticularity for particularity); the assured confidence traded for a lean vulnerability; the unlit cigarette in the mouth once coded as style traded for smoke captured as a screen. What is remarkable is how the smoke assumes the shape of a mask, objectifying for a moment the transitory shifts in identity that his business specialized in. The image contrasts the traditional view of masculine identity as fixed with a presentation of personal identity as fluid, open to the imagination for change, although reliant on the accoutrements of style to effect this. To understand the way in which this construction of fashionable identity operated, we need to know not only about the growth of the organization, but also the clientele, which can be graded and identified in relation to the exposure and success of the John Stephen enterprise.

Retailing and Window Display

As stated, John Stephen inherited his initial custom from his previous employer, Bill Green. Green was a physique photographer who had branched into retailing separates on the back of a success found in selling unusually colored men's briefs. Catering largely to butch gay trade (the Marsham Street baths and gym were local, as was the Palladium Theatre), Vince's sold a range of Continental styles: imported American blue denim jeans, black turtlenecks reputedly from the Left Bank, Italianate hipster-cut trousers, and Greek fishing caps. The unusual items, often fashioned in unconventional fabrics, began to attract select custom, and famed individuals gradually began to patronize the shop.

John Stephen took Vince's as a model for his shop, but realized that the key to transforming the scale of the operation was to involve heterosexual young men as a key to diffusing the transition of essentially homosexual dress into the fashion mainstream as a modern and optimistic trend, unbounded by sexual orientation. This was largely achieved by Stephen's undercutting Vince's market, as he realized that most teenagers couldn't afford to shop there.

Stephen was to take advantage of the techniques of advertising "drag" goods through veiled terms—often a combination of innocuous model poses with a suggestively worded narrative in the underground gay press, translating the style for an emerging media that served the teenage consumer market. Instead of nameless models, Stephen used his famous clientele; instead of innuendo, information was typed on the back of the press photograph on the star's latest pursuits. Much of this was secured by Mike McGrath, a pop group photographer and women's magazine journalist who helped cement Stephen's constant good relations with the media. Their first success was a photograph of British boxing hope Billy Walker in tight-fitting slacks and a striped matelot shirt in 1962 (modeling with a young Caroline Neville). The photograph was blown up and used as backdrop to the window displays in all the shops. In terms of the codes of window display for men's shops, it was revolutionary to see a heterosexual boxer of considerable repute modeling what was considered "drag" clothing.

Music was established as an active component of the shops, as was an attention to detail in window display and interior design. John Stephen was one of the first to identify these elements as a factor in encouraging men to shop for pleasure, and assigned the tasks to in-house display artist Anthony Myers, in a move typical of the new cachet accorded to professions previously thought of as down-at-heel, "their slightest activity being faithfully described in newspapers and magazines, several of the latter existing, on glossy paper, solely for this purpose, and their slightest word being no less faithfully recorded, the words of some of them being slight indeed" (Booker 1969: 282).

Inside the initial spaces Scandinavian-style blond slatted false ceilings hung next to fine Italianate ironwork arches, while black and white vinyl tiles hinted at Venetian stone. Each element was presented not in terms of an overall design, but as a series of applied effects reminiscent of those utilized in stage design. Blown-up photographs of Piranesi's graphic works were employed for their strong, structural and masculine decorative associations—a visual style that nodded to classical beauty while referencing the modern Italianate vogue in its rendering.

At this point, the Continentally-derived style was imported in much the same way as the casual separates. They were recognized as lexicons of travel, leisure and unconventional sophistication, and were used to frame the new masculine experience of shopping for clothes as a participatory act. More interestingly, they helped to mask the movement of the mirror from the changing-room to the shop floor. Mirror walls were often the main feature of the designed interior, not only for the customer's reflection but also to give the illusion of space in what were cramped retail spaces. The disguising and transmutation of what was essentially a communal mirror into an aspect of the interior design meant that self-awareness was no longer an isolated experience, but something played out in a context that architecturally echoed the street.

The strong recognition of change in the London landscape of the 1960s was a motivational factor in the belief in accelerated progress. More than any other material, the architectural use of the glass curtain became symbolic of self-awareness both in its transparency and in its ability to reflect. The mimicking of this in the use of plate mirror in shop design could be construed as parody; but at this point parody was restrained, almost pared-down—suggestive of naiveté. For parody was formulated not in the interior, nor in dress, but in window display.

The example of the artist Robyn Denny's mural of 1959 for Austin Reed's flagship store in Regent Street is particularly relevant here, as it was commissioned in response to the growing threat of nearby Carnaby Street and its youth styles to middle-market menswear, well represented in Regent Street. (It wasn't until 1961 that John Stephen opened the first "official" boutique for men on Regent Street.) Denny's brief as a recently graduated painter from the Royal College of Art was to engage the new consumer market and modernize the company image by "adopting the signs of metropolitan novelty." His mural was a red, white and blue typographic collage of words that screamed the frenetic jargon of advertising and celebrated London as "GREAT, BIG, WIDE, BIGGEST!"

To make sense of how this impacted upon a sense of the marketing and design of Swinging London, one should consider the design as reordering the visual grammar of a national symbol to present an understanding of the metropolitan landscape as fractured and complex. The Austin Reed mural took the traditional forms of advertising and display that promoted London and represented them to the discerning, knowledgeable metropolitan consumer. It was concerned with reconfiguring the known cultural landscape with irreverence in a slightly self-congratulatory manner. Most importantly, it was for the home market—not for the tourist gaze. In combination, the language of advertising London and the Union Jack flag became visual emblems of new London, hijacked and interpreted in less imaginistic ways for window display. This is the crux: without the artistic intervention, the emblems became merely representative; without graphic distortion they were recognizable, guiding tourist experience rather than reformulating it.

The importance of the role of window display for Swinging London was based, not in the capital, but in America, with the concurrent rise of Beatlemania. (It is curiously apt that one of the Beatles' first London photo-sessions in 1963 was in front of the Austin Reed mural.) The marketed imagery of the Beatles in America was largely complemented by the traditional icons of tourist London: Bobbie hats, traffic signs, Union Jack flags, Trooping the Color. The literal quality of their presentation was in order for American eyes to understand them. The obviousness of the reproduction of the symbols of the street was intended to ease the tourists' passage; what it also succeeded in doing was confusing them.

It is at this point that the American misunderstanding of the word "mod" becomes particularly poignant. According to Jonathan Green "what had been an English invention had taken on the appearance of its American Equivalent. Mod in America had only meant 'modern'. It was applied slapdash to anything new and shiny and supposedly young" (Green 1998: 74). This would include elements as arbitrary as Lord Snowdon, Carnaby Street, restaurants, Mary Quant, nightclubs and Vidal Sassoon. Although all were elements of a social and cultural framework developing around London, they bore no relation to the set of consumers who frequented John Stephen and defined a subcultural identity. In invention's becoming appearance, the coded qualities of the mods' patterns of consumption were appropriated and diluted into a surface that could be applied, like a veneer, to a range of other phenomena. It is the American media's process of turning subcultural modes of consumption, dress and behavior into a model for reporting on aspects of metropolitan creativity and living that is particularly pertinent. The opening of John Stephen's first shop for girls, Trécamp prompted an article in the *New York Herald Tribune*:

> It's Trécamp—even if the salesgirls don't know what that means. You can't blame them too much either, Trécamp being a combination of *trés* (French for very) and *camp* (American for, well, camp) . . . Inside the changing rooms are not the usual mirrors, but three blow-up, life size pictures of boys. Handsome boys, who are what's more, in various states of undress. One, a blond Adonis type (and an art student in real life) is bare-chested and is sliding down his trunks zipper (which, however is placed sideways) while giving you a full, toothy smile. In the second sitting room, there is a slightly built and what the English call sweet-looking boy, in trunks again and taking off—no, not his trunks—but his shirt, and looking at you in a sort of sad and deadpan way. The boy is the lead singer in a new beat group called "The Carnaby." (*New York Herald Tribune* 20/10/1965)

Trécamp was Stephen's response to the ever-growing demand for his clothes from women, who favored the casual, androgynous styles. What is relevant is how the shop's interior decoration parodied that of those in the street catering to men and, in doing so, became a cause for concern for the American journalist—much horrified by Anthony Myers's proclamation that the mannequins in the window display were "bisexual. Their bosoms and wigs come off—and we can use them in the boys' stores too." The interchangeable nature of the look was indicative of a diluted formula and an economy of means rather than of any attempt at a sexual revolution in window display such as the article was keen to attest to. Still, the interior decoration made the news on the other side of the Atlantic.

It was at this point that Stephen expanded his empire, opening concessions in department stores in New York, Minneapolis and Chicago, while concentrating his stores in Britain only in the central London area, hoping to maximize the association with the capital to boost overseas sales, which he saw as key to the company's expansion. This was not without its problems:

> [In America] the masculine look is like a religion. Their shoes haunt me—they're like mountaineering boots. But the Americans want everything that's new, immediately I put it on the market. They're on the phone to me every day from Chicago and Minneapolis . . .

"God-damn, John, where are our flowered ties?" Then I worry about flowered ties with mountaineering boots (*TitBits*, 1.1.1966).

Mods in Three Stages

Farid Chenoune (1993) identifies the three stages of mod (both as a youth subculture and a style of dress) as "modernist" between 1958 and 1961, "mod" between 1961 and 1963 and "modest" (referring to those on tight budgets and of a pack mentality) between 1963 and 1966. I will refer later to the role of the Individualists, a case of modernists post-mod, and their influence in changing a metropolitan notion of style.

The modernists, named for their liking of modern as opposed to traditional jazz, derived pleasure from the consumption of rarefied commodities including imported black vinyl, imported white Ivy-League shirts, tailor-made mohair and silk suits and custom-made shoes. With a quickly established code of narcissism, they identified the act of consumption as a self-conscious pursuit that one should spend time on and be seen partaking of. Because of this, a shop such as John Stephen's relinquished its role as an insular affair for a select clientele and became a space of commerce that engaged the street and propositioned passers-by. Thus Carnaby Street entered into its modern incarnation with a brief episode of "authentic" goods, "considered" consumption, "real" street culture and undiscovered, almost illicit pleasures. Snippets of press editorials from the period show an adolescent and as yet unknown Mick Jagger and Keith Richards photographed, lost in the contemplation of a purchase nestling inside a John Stephen paper bag.

The devaluing of the term "mod" was not confined to America, but was becoming manifest in the clothes of the Carnaby Street boutiques. Mod clothing had always possessed an ironic stance towards established social values, parodying smartness to the point of obsessiveness. But the evolution of mod style in terms of retailing on Carnaby Street changed that. The mods gave John Stephen the fast beat of consumption that he matched; Stephen was able to supply a continual differentiated range of stock that could keep up with the weekly changes, the weekend dances and the weekly charts. The problem was in regenerating the original array of casual, separate styles.

It is generally agreed that around 1965, as with other areas of pop culture, the demand for ever-evolving newness forced a distraction from innovation and invention towards a plundering and interpretation of historical styles. This can also be understood in terms of a simplification of codes and details, often reduced down to the lowest common denominator. In terms of menswear, an obvious example would be a shift from the Union Jack flag jacket (as worn by The Who) to the adoption of military uniform as emblematic of a disregard for the establishment. Stephen's responded to the speed of the market by adapting designs from other sources: Italy was exchanged for India, op and pop exchanged for the nostalgic and foppish.

A press photograph from September 1964 captures this approach in its infancy. It depicts John Stephen in a sharply-cut suit holding the hand of a shop mannequin dressed in nineteenth-century military uniform whose other hand is held by a model wearing thin trousers and a striped cotton kurta. Although the intention behind the image is now lost, we do know that, on first coming to London, Stephen worked in the military department at Moss Bros. However, to see both Indian and military influences in men's dress being brought together nearly two years before they acquired their counter-cultural connotations is indicative of a naive playing on historical and cultural styles in a bid to proclaim difference and attract fashion.

> In the effort never to lose speed or excitement, he got stuck in the visual equivalent of triple forte. All subtleties were forgotten, any possible pleasure of texture or line. Instead, there was automatic frenzy. Each new style was made wilder, more gimmicky than the

Figure 2
John Stephen of London Group, advertising campaign, "The Brightest street in London has just had another idea," as published in *The Times*, 26 August 1968. Broad equal border of original design lost to clipping. Reproduced with the permission of V&A Picture Library.

> one before; each window screamed louder than its neighbor. In no time, a limit had been reached and, from then on, the effect was like a jammed car-horn, blaring so ceaselessly and mindlessly that one doesn't even hear it. (Cohn 1971: 70)

Cohn's description interestingly fuses Stephen's marketing policy with the spectacle of the street. In reaching its limit, Stephen's array of goods for sale became transformed into a shrill effect, sounding beyond the ears of its original consumers to those far, far away. Thus the effect became the spectacle, rather than the consumers, or the clothes. All that remained was for the tourists to see the spectacle, and the product for sale to become the souvenir. At this point the clothing shifts from being clothing consumed by mods into modernity clothed as consumption. Surprisingly, this is echoed at the time in John Stephen's advertising. A magazine advertisement in *Queen* from 1968 depicts a group of people reading a map with the attached copy: "Carnaby Street. When John Stephen found it twelve years ago, it was just a tiny turning tucked behind Regent Street . . . Come and see. Particularly if you're looking for Regent Street. It's tucked just behind Carnaby Street" (*Queen*: October 1968).

Instead of communicating ideas about the latest men's fashions, the advertisement communicates the legacy of male fashion in post-war London, pitting the fame of Carnaby Street against the middle-market majority of Regent Street. Yet, in exchanging the image of the fashionable male for the unfashionable tourist, any sense of the original innovation is lost. This was the predicament that John Stephen actively embraced: a fame that alienated his original clientele. For even though the mods expressed themselves primarily as consumers, they were ruined by the commercialism of Carnaby Street, and their intentions led them elsewhere.

Carnaby St. and the Notion of the Street

In being labeled "King of Carnaby Street" John Stephen suffered from a very particular relationship with the reputation of the street, something now tangible and not merely a media invention. By the mid-sixties, the street sign had become the best-selling London tourist postcard, an attraction to rival any other. Capitalizing on the worldwide interest in Swinging London, Carnaby Street became the only tangible destination for those keen to participate in a slice of the action. To this end, the purpose of the street was to dazzle: "Salesmen grabbed you and cajoled you like pimps. Colored streamers were festooned above the pavements and the clothes were like showgirl lipsticks: flaming orange, cherry red, candyfloss pink" (Cohn 1974: 112).

The ephemerality of the look had become too enwrapped in the instant and the disposable, appealing far more to the needs of the daytripper than to the discerning consumer. The charge of crass commercialism leveled at Carnaby Street was not unjustified: record marketing executives had even tried to popularize an invented dance called the Carnaby. John Stephen responded by seriously launching the Beau Brummell award for best-dressed personality of the year.

His final riposte was to move beyond the concept of the boutique and embrace the department store. After 1966 Stephen sold all his shops outside Carnaby Street, downscaling from twenty to eight on the road he believed he had begun. Instead of gimmicks, he embraced principles. By the late 1960s, the dress of youth culture had dissolved into a disarray of kaftans and a kind of Regency brocade. In addition, the innovations that the modernists had made in men's dress were having populist repercussions: "Thousands of British fathers have been bashfully copying their son's sense of dress in an attempt to keep up with modern trends—and have knocked the bottom out of the mod market. But worse. Dad just hasn't queered the teenage pitch, he's also making a mess of himself" (*Daily Express* 16/4/1970).

Stephen's response was to cut out the flamboyance and concentrate on "fairly sober trend-conscious clothes" (*Queen*, July 1969), which included the reintroduction of the three-piece suit. Flamboyance was to reassert itself in and around Savile Row, led by Micheal Fish, a former Assistant Managing Director at John Stephen who was backed by Barry Sainsbury. "The market has now neatly reversed itself. As Carnaby Street sobers, the wildest fashions come from the top end of the trade—Mr Fish and Blades—where prices rocket and the customers are by no means teenagers" (*Scottish Daily Mail* 19/04/1969). Micheal Fish and Rupert Lycett-Green distanced themselves from youth by price and the prestige of location, whereas John Stephen attempted to do this by policy. He emphasized shop design, service, color range, and choice, famously offering a shirt in 50 colors. As the advertisement in *The Times* read: "In Carnaby Street, the bright ideas are no longer necessarily the brightest. Hanging around all the happy hippy youthful gear you can now find quieter clothes. Cut with the flair of John Stephen designs—but gently" (*The Times* 26/8/1968). The copy was accompanied by a photograph of models posing as a professional couple, clearly indicating that Stephen was interested in upgrading his customer base by dealing in luxury product. Yet by this time London already possessed a shopping area outside of Savile Row that had gained a reputation for supplying clothes with flair to the discerning male consumer.

The Chelsea Set

Carnaby Street was only one shopping area that was transformed by the emergence of the idea of Swinging London. The King's Road in Chelsea was, most famously, the setting for Mary Quant's assault on women's fashion conducted with her husband Alexander Plunket-Greene from the shop Bazaar, opened in 1955. Yet the King's Road was very much more than a shopping zone, being home not only to the "Chelsea Set," but also an "ambience." Christopher Booker claimed this ambience to be expressive of "the point where the hereditary attitudes of the upper and upper-middle class young were most obviously crumbling into a new freedom, the ambience that was to be associated with Chelsea bistros and the glossy magazines and John Michael shirts from the Kings' Road" (Booker 1969: 143).

This statement proves a link between certain isolated consumables and certain class-identified consumers. Although the intent behind such associations is not obvious, the geographical specificity is. As Mary Quant recounted in her autobiography: "Nobody has ever been able to make up his mind precisely what the 'Chelsea Set' was but I think it grew out of something in the air which developed into a serious attempt to break away from the Establishment" (Quant 1966: 80). For Quant, her youthful designs were not intended to challenge the divisions of class in dress (her clothes were supposedly bought by the daughters of dukes and the daughters of dock workers), but were intended to emphasize the distinction between her generation and her mother's. The paradox was that the emphasis that the designs put on making young women look like little girls (or dolly girls) was what made them problematic for the establishment.

Quant was a key figure of the "New Aristocracy," but her inclusion was not merely for her creativity, but for her positioning. Quant was reared in South London, identified by Booker as part of the Young (Creative) Urban Lower Class that also included John Stephen. However, owing to her marriage to Eton-educated Plunket-Greene and the location of her business, she was accorded alternative status. This raises questions about the possibility of class characteristics' being embedded in retail areas. The possible sedimentation of upper-middle-class values residing in Chelsea as a retailing area is underlined by the presence of Terence Conran's pre-digested shopping experience Habitat, opened in the King's Road in 1964 and other shops, including Alice Pollock's Quorum, Michael Rainey's Hung on You and Nigel Weymouth's Granny Takes A Trip.

In terms of a masculine identity being reconciled with the area, this was provided by a kind of *louche* dandyism promoted by Christopher Gibbs, then editor of *Vogue for Men*. Very much an individualist, Gibbs is credited with being the first man to sport flares in 1961 and with ordering flower print shirts as early as 1964. Yet, for all his innovations in masculine dress, Gibbs and his circle "remained traditionalist in that they very much cared about quality. They were Pop, certainly; but they weren't popular, meaning common, and they had nothing but scorn for Carnaby Street and its tattiness. 'Trash,' says David Mlinaric. 'Always was, and it still is'" (Cohn 1971: 93).

Even though this group of individuals originally patronized Blades (run by an Etonian shopkeeper) when it was located in Dover Street (in the

Savile Row area) they colonized Chelsea and Kensington for their rich and civilized connotations. By the opening of Hung on You in 1965, they began an innovation in men's dress that initiated the descent into the hippy vogue for anti-taste and solidified a masculine identity in opposition to that of Carnaby Street. This is well demonstrated by an article in *Life* magazine in July 1966 titled "So Long Sad Sack" that analyzed developments in men's dress in London, Paris and Chicago, but with a firm emphasis on London as being central to the rejection of the staid suit:

> It all began with the teen-age "mods" (*Life International* July 27, 1961) who spent most of their money on flamboyant clothes. Now the frills and flowers are being adopted in other strata of Britain's society . . . London's fashion revolution is not all teen-agers and pop singers in op-arty tie and thigh-high boots. A new aristocratic tailoring establishment such as Blades is being influenced by the Carnaby Street look. The Chelsea shops offer several elegant variations on the new attire such as a 1920s silent movie look and an increasingly popular Edwardian look. (*Life*: July 1966)

As a whole, the article strongly adheres to the style of American reporting discussed earlier (a good example being the statement that Blades was influenced by the Carnaby Street look). It presents two oppositional themes over two spreads, which, although manifesting some inaccuracies, help to confirm the presence of two masculine style positions to be found in London, differentiated by class and location. The first presented John Stephen with models posing around a Cadillac on Carnaby Street, The Kinks in a studio shot with the lyrics to "Dedicated Follower of Fashion" printed underneath, and Nigel Weymouth standing outside Granny Takes a Trip with Michael Chaplin (son of Charlie Chaplin). This inaccuracy (Granny Takes a Trip was decidedly Chelsea) is underlined by the copy: "One secret of [their] success is the determination of London's young men to dress differently than their bowler-hatted elders." In total, the layout places emphasis on vitality, solidarity, a rejection of convention and a straight-off-the-peg newness.

The second spread documents the actor David Hemmings trying on a jacket in Blades; the Duke of Bedford in his Canaletto Room; Ossie Clark, Nigel Winterbottom and Michael Williams in a Chelsea pub; and Christopher Gibbs, "a leader of Chelsea's chic bluebloods, wear[ing] a silk and lace shirt and Renoir like hat—an overall 1900 allure." Here, the oppositional values of privilege, tradition and order are asserted, most tellingly in Gibbs's proclamation: "We encouraged friends to dig into their heirlooms, to wear old clothes, to turn their backs on ugliness and conformism."

This use of old clothing as an indicator of noble descent became important as an indicator of taste and status; but this was also mirrored in a wider and more accessible vogue still enshrined in the Chelsea area.

Barbara Hulanicki of Biba was reported as saying: "'I love old things. Modern things are so cold. I need things that have lived.' Baffling words for such a 'with it' designer . . . with everything around her so fast, so uncertain, she needs to go home to . . . the comfort of dark red wallpaper and Edwardiana. It makes her feel safe" (*The Daily Telegraph* 27/10/1966).

Hulanicki's responding to the maddening modern environment by having recourse to old things was symptomatic of cultural changes unbound by location. The developing apotheosis of the Beatles towards mysticism and the influence of Ashbury Heights shifted youth culture and dress into a different direction. In terms of perception this moved from "uppers" (a sharp, excited, amphetamine thrill) to "downers" (a loose, blissful, hashish buzz). It could also be defined as moving from the world of working-class mods to that of middle-class hippies, a gendered shift towards a more feminine style and a move in dress from a position of taste to one of anti-taste. However, beyond youth culture, taste was being reasserted in the realms of magazine publishing and consumerism to redefine "The New Class."

The Taste-making Individualists

The pop revolution first showed us that The New Class had arrived. But now our three-year love affair with the Pop scene is crumbling at the edges. The pop stars and the dolly look, after a vacuous dictatorship of our mass-media and style of life, are being handed back to the teen-groups from whom they sprung. Is The New Class finished along with the Beatle/Bailey cult? Not Yet. They are preparing their next move. (*Queen* 14 July 1965)

The next move was to raise distinctions within a media phenomenon that had previously been described as classless. This was achieved by moving away from associations with youth as an indicator of vitality and embracing a rarefied, metropolitan knowledge of "Who? Why? Where? When?" The index pages of *Queen* displayed in tabular form the "Yes" and "No" answers to a range of issues such as "Artists to have at your party," "Discothèques," "Bistros," "Women's hairdressers" and "Men's Clubs." John Stephen's custom-built tailoring was a "No," while Blades for shirts was a "Yes" (*Queen* 14 July 1965). Swelling expressions of personal identity into what Jonathan Raban considered "a new pornography of taste" (Raban 1974: 66), the development attracted former modernists who had become disillusioned with what their elemental identity had become aligned with. For many of them, it was the realization that newness was no longer required as a badge of modernity, and that this was replaced by the value of taste, largely effected through arbitrary changes in the value of commodities. In placing themselves as affective to these changes they can be considered as early exponents of what we now term stylists.

Jonathan Raban's influential reading of a city as being defined by the "Soft City" (1974) of the mind rather than the hard city located in structures and maps defined this kind of activity as the Moroccan birdcage syndrome (Moroccan birdcage painted white being a stylistic *objet d'art* for the interior in the early 1970s.) Raban claimed it as being:

> A useful model for a certain kind of industrial process—a process which both supplies a demand for commodities whose sole feature is their expressiveness of taste, and becomes, by virtue of its laws of economic transformation, the ultimate arbiter of that taste. The stylistic entrepreneurs who make their living out of this curious trade go, along with gangsters and dandies, into the bracket of people possessed of a special kind of city knowledge. (Raban 1974: 102)

In terms of the selling of men's dress, this can be related to developments spearheaded in the early 1970s by entrepreneurs such as Tommy Roberts, who ran Mr. Freedom, a boutique that ransacked the 1930s for Hollywood glamor and mixed it with a poppy, garish aesthetic typified by a T-shirt appliquéd with a large glitter star; or his former partner Trevor Miles, who opened Paradise Garage, the first shop in London to import American second-hand vintage denims for sale. Raban's observation that these people possessed a "special kind of city knowledge" echoes observations made earlier about the symbols of the street and the Union Jack flag's being used in window dressing to promote the consumption of men's dress in the early 1960s. The coded qualities of these commodities are, of course, central to what we are dealing with; but in terms of John Stephen's position in relation to this knowledge at this point, fashion had moved on.

A publicity drive in 1969 celebrated a well-worn theme: "Why not be patriotic when it packs a fashion punch? For whoever designed the British Flag probably gave no thought to the fact that red, white and blue make one of the striking color combinations in clothes" (*Boutique*: June 1969). In directional terms, patriotism was the last thing on the mind of the fashionable male, who was now far more interested in the vogue for Continental labels such as Cerruti, Palazzi and Newman that gave an air of understatement long missing in male dress.

Carnaby Street now required no "special kind of city knowledge" to navigate or consume, and the attempt to transform its tired emblems into another guise of fashionability is symptomatic of Stephen's protective defence of his invention, but ultimately, of how he had lost contact with the young fashionable male that was once his customer. When being interviewed for Nik Cohn's 1971 book *Today There Are No Gentlemen* he looked out of his office window on to Carnaby Street "'Who are they?' said John Stephen, smiling his sorrowful smile. 'They're nobody in particular; they're Mister Average.' One day, presumably, it was bound

Figure 3
Victor Burgin, poster, "What does possession mean to you?," 1976, photograph Geoff Dunlop. Reproduced with the kind permission of the artist and photographer.

to collapse . . . 'The street itself may go,' said Stephen. 'The changes it made will still be there.'" In 1975 John Stephen and his partner Bill Frank sold their stakes in the John Stephen of London group and the business closed. In the following year the artist Victor Burgin created a photographic poster for flyposting, depicting a couple embracing, with the caption "What does possession mean to you? 7% of our population own 84% of our wealth." Burgin was part of a new breed of politically motivated artists keen to critique advertising for its role in capitalist consumption. The style of the poster was meant to be innocuous and merely ape recognizable formats. The closeness of the layout to those of John Stephen's late advertising campaigns calls into question the shift in a business from one that communicated fashionability through its close relation to the style of the street to one that communicated fashionability through advertising campaigns directed at an elite minority who no longer wished to be associated with the street. It implies that "possession" clearly meant two very different things to the two different types of male consumers. For the modernists, possession was something to be played out in the street; for the stylists, possession was something to secure away from the street. To the misfortune of John Stephen, possession in this context was neither wanted by Mr. Average nor Mr. "7%." This confirms Green's observation about the "classless revolution" that John Stephen and his business were so much a part of: "for Swinging London equality was never the point" (Green 1998: 81).

Acknowledgments

I would like to thank Michael Talboys and Christopher Breward for their assistance with this article.

References

Bailey, David. 1999. *David Bailey: Archive One*. London: Thames & Hudson.

Benson, Richard. 1999. ". . . and that's how I felt about the gas cape, dad. A personal history of Carnaby Street." In *Shopping*. London: FAT.

Booker, Christopher. 1969. *The Neophiliacs*. London: Collins.

Chenoune, Farid. 1993. *A History of Men's Dress*. Paris: Flammarion.

Cohn, Nik. 1971. *Today There Are No Gentlemen: The Changes in Englishmen's Clothes Since the War*. Birkenhead: Willmer Brothers Ltd.

Craik, Jennifer. 1993. *The Face of Fashion*. New York, London: Routledge.

Goddard, Donald. 1972. *Blimey! Another Book about London*. London: Cassell & Collier Macmillan.

Green, Jonathan. 1998. *Days in the Life: Voices from the English Underground 1961–1971*. London: Pimlico Press.

——. 1998. *All Dressed Up*. London: Pimlico Press.

John Stephen archive, Archive of Art & Design. Victoria & Albert Museum, London.

McDowell, Colin. 1997. *The Man of Fashion: Peacock Males and Perfect Gentlemen*. London: Thames & Hudson.

de Marly, Diana. 1985. *Fashion for Men: An Illustrated History*. London: Batsford.

Melly, George. 1970. *Revolt into Style: The Pop Arts in Britain*. London: Allen Lane/Penguin Press.

Mort, Frank. 1996. *Cultures of Consumption: Masculinities and Social Space in Late Twentieth-Century Britain*. London: Routledge.

Porter, Roy. 1994. *London: A Social History*. London: Hamish Hamilton.

Quant, Mary. 1966. *Quant on Quant*. London.

Raban, Jonathan. 1974. *Soft City*. London: Hamish Hamilton.

The Sixties in Queen. 1987. Edited by Nicholas Coleridge and Stephen Quinn. London: Ebury Press.

Stern, Jane and Michael Stern. 1990. *Sixties People*. London: Macmillan.

Wheen, Francis. 1982. *The Sixties: A Fresh Look at the Decade of Change*. London: Century Publishing.

Fashion Theory, Volume 4, Issue 4, pp.507–508
Reprints available directly from the Publishers.
Photocopying permitted by licence only.

Reviewed by
Valerie Steele

Book Review

***The Hidden Consumer: Masculinities, fashion and city life 1860–1914*, Christopher Breward. Manchester University Press, 1999**

Christopher Breward's previous book *The Culture of Fashion* (Manchester University Press, 1995) went beyond descriptive costume history to present a more sophisticated example of the new fashion scholarship. Within the framework of the chronological survey, Breward addressed issues such as class and gender, sexual and identity politics, consumerism and modernity. It was and remains an extremely useful text for students, because it laid out the methodological and theoretical issues in an accessible form.

Breward continues his cultural analysis of fashion in *The Hidden Consumer: Masculinities, fashion and city life 1860–1914*, which focuses on the consuming habits of urban men, and on the ways in which sexual and class identities are expressed through clothing. The period under examination has been identified as crucial to the emergence of commodity culture, but research has hitherto focused almost entirely on the female consumer. In texts ranging from the now-classic history of kleptomania, *When Ladies Go A' Thieving*, to recent histories, such as *Consuming Angels* and *The Pleasures of Shopping*, we see women shop, shoplift, dress up and fashion new modern identities. But men, it seems, were busy doing other, masculine things. Breward, however, provides ample evidence to the contrary.

Six years of in-depth research into a wide variety of source material have unearthed tailoring magazines, family budgets, handbills, trade catalogs, advertisements, as well as long-forgotten books with titles such as *Young Gaol Birds* and *Manchester Boys: Sketches of Manchester Lads at Work and Play*. These sources enable Breward to make a convincing case that male patterns of consumption were intimately linked to the emergence of modern masculine identities. Although dense, his book contains a wealth of fascinating material, which other scholars and students are sure to pillage for years to come. Stereotypes are modified or demolished, as Breward shows, for example, that the notorious "great masculine renunciation" has been greatly exaggerated, if we consider just how flashy and raffish young men could be. In contrast to the elitist tendencies of traditional dress history, Breward details the clothing of the urban working classes.

Especially interesting is his analysis of the language of sartorial pleasure: "saucy cut togs . . . slap up with the artful dodge . . . fancy skin kicksies . . . Lavenders, built spanky . . . made to flash the dicky, from 9 bob. A discount made to prize fighters . . .." As he notes, many of these terms derive from "the vulgar language of aristocratic debauchery associated with [an] earlier period of dandyism" [p. 156]. Breward is also astute in analyzing the semiotics of what he calls "subversive performances," whereby the mode of self-presentation asssociated with bachelor role-models found distorted reflections in the styles of other would-be fashionable young men. As Breward observes, some of the cockney promenaders of 1914 were "as sharp and self-aware as any Colin MacInnes character from fifty years later" [p. 208]. Anyone interested in male impersonators, musclemen, dandies, gentlemen, Ally Sloper or Oscar Wilde will find something in this book.

Fashion Theory, Volume 4, Issue 4, pp.509–510
Reprints available directly from the Publishers.
Photocopying permitted by licence only.

Annual Index

Articles

Book Reviews